Andrew Woods
Grace Romano

Oxford Grammar

Third Edition

Name: ______________________

Class: ______________________

6

OXFORD
UNIVERSITY PRESS

Contents

Topic 1: Nouns, adjectives and noun groups

Topic 2: Verbs, adverbs and prepositional phrases

Topic 3: Text cohesion and language devices

Topic 4: Sentences, clauses, conjunctions, direct and indirect speech and apostrophes

Topic 5: Using grammar to enrich your writing

Topic 6: Enrichment and revision

Topic 1: Nouns, adjectives and noun groups

Learning intention

We are learning to use a variety of nouns, adjectives and noun groups to add more precise, varied and engaging information about people, places and things.

Unit 1.1 Common nouns

The day my bum went psycho

Zack Freeman woke out of a deep sleep to see his bum perched on the ledge of his bedroom window. It was standing on two pudgy little legs, silhouetted against the moon, its little stick-like arms outstretched in front of it, as if it was about to dive.

Zack sat up in bed.

"No!" he yelled. "Come back!"

But it was too late. His bum jumped out of the window and landed with a soft thud in the garden bed below.

Zack stared at the window and sighed.

"Oh no," he said. "Not again."

This was not the first time Zack's bum had run away.

Since his twelfth birthday, two months ago, Zack's bum had made a habit of jumping off his body and running around the streets making a nuisance of itself. Zack was sick of it. So was the local bumcatcher, who had already caught and impounded it three times.

Until recently, Zack's bum had confined itself to a variety of harmless pranks, such as attaching itself to the faces of statues and passersby. But on its last outing it had joined a pack of five hundred feral bums who had lined the emergency stopping lane of the South Eastern Freeway and mooned all the people driving to work. This stunt had caused many accidents, which the bums had thought was a great laugh. The sentencing judge, however, was not amused and placed them all on twelve month good behaviour bonds.

Zack knew he had to catch his bum himself this time. If the bumcatcher got involved, he would have to report it and Zack's bum would end up in jail for sure. And there was no way Zack wanted to spend every second weekend visiting his bum in jail.

Andy Griffiths

A common noun is a word used to name ordinary things. For example: *table, tree, egg*

1 Write common nouns from "The day my bum went psycho", using these clues.

a A piece of furniture where Zack was sleeping: ____________

b The part of the house where Zack's bum landed: ____________

c The person who catches runaway bums: ____________

d The part of statues and passers-by that Zack's bum attached itself to: ____________

e The place where Zack's bum joined a pack of feral bums: ____________

f The thing the bums' prank caused: ____________

g The person who sentenced the feral bums: ____________

There is a noun for every person, creature, place, thing, idea, feeling or quality (such as intelligence). Everything that exists can be named using a noun.

Common nouns only begin with capital letters if they are used to begin a sentence.

2 Write a sentence for each of these common nouns.

a statue ____________

b window ____________

3 Write five common nouns for each group.

a living creatures ____________

b things that fly ____________

Try it out!

On a separate piece of paper, sort the **common nouns** below into the categories shown on the right.

Common nouns

sadness	saucepan	courage
soldier	zoo	thought
shark	teacher	love
curiosity	dragon	anger
home	flower	jealousy
octopus	pencil	justice

Categories

person	quality
creature	idea
place	feeling
thing	

Monday blues

Cornflakes were soggy.
Cat licked my egg.
On the school bus
got thumped by Greg.

Sprung again talking
before morning bell –
that Mr Moore can
sure make life hell!

Ticked off for homework –
half out of ten.
Had to miss recess
and do it again.

Strife in mathematics
with Mr Moore.
Sent out to stand in
the corridor.

Looking for battle
came Tracey Frost.
She packs a wallop!
(So guess who lost.)

Biro leaked black ink
on my new jeans.
Soggy fish sandwich
instead of baked beans.

In art and craft room
upset the glue.
Half in my pocket,
the rest in my shoe.

Afternoon playtime,
Shane (my ex-mate)
spread it around that
I fancy Kate.

Practised my footie,
kicked ball quite far.
Guess where it landed?
Mr Moore's car.

Kept in for giggling.
Got home real late.
No wonder bears choose
to hibernate!

by arrangement with
Robin Klein, c/– Curtis Brown
(Aust) Pty Ltd

Common nouns name ordinary things. For example, in "Monday blues", some of the common nouns that have been used are *bell*, *ball*, *recess*, *battle* and *pocket*.

1 Use a noun from the box to describe each group of common nouns.

food   animals   transport   clothing

a bears fish cat ____________________
b jeans shoe scarf ____________________
c sandwich baked beans egg ________
d car bus bike ____________________

Proper nouns are special names of people, places, things or ideas. A proper noun always begins with a capital letter.

2 Write five proper nouns from the poem "Monday blues" that are the names of people.

____

____

____

Some nouns can be **abstract nouns.** They are names for things that you cannot see or touch. For example: **fear**, **pity**, **fun**, **fury**, **idea**, **beauty**, **length**, **duty**, **dancing**

3 Find and write these common or proper nouns from the poem.

a schoolwork done at home ________________
b brand of cereal ____________________
c a passageway ____________________
d a feline animal ____________________
e a teacher at the school ________________
f the writer's ex-friend ____________________

4 Write proper nouns to match the statements.

a Usually I am the first day of the school week. ________________________
b the capital city of Australia ________________________
c the highest mountain in Australia ________________________
d the city of the 2028 Olympic Games ________________________

5 Write collective nouns that would be used for these groups.

a sheep ______________
b bees ______________
c football players ______
d bananas ______________

A collective noun names a group of people, places, animals, things or ideas.
For example: *a* ***bunch*** *of grapes, a* ***pack*** *of wolves, a* ***fleet*** *of ships*

Try it out!

Here are some unusual ***collective nouns***: *a* ***clowder*** *of cats, a* ***murder*** *of crows, a* ***knot*** *of toads, a* ***smack*** *of jellyfish, a* ***parliament*** *of owls, a* ***business*** *of ferrets*. Imagine that you have been given the job of coming up with collective nouns for the following groups. On a separate piece of paper, write your suggestions.

a A ... of clowns
b A ... of dragons
c A ... of racing cars
d A ... of slugs
e A ... of politicians
f A ... of mobile phone users

The young castaways

Once upon a time, a group of young adventurers arrived on Adventure Isle to participate in the ultimate challenge: Young Survivor. These brave kids, all around 11 years old, were called "castaways" and had to live on the island, providing food, water, fire and shelter for themselves.

The castaways were:

- Lalita, the clever leader
- Mia, the brave explorer
- Ravi, the strong builder
- Suyin, the knowledgeable healer
- Jace, the agile scout
- Ava, the imaginative problem-solver.

The host, Mr Adventure, explained the rules: "You will face challenges to earn rewards and immunity from elimination. Each week, one of you will be voted off the island. The last one standing will be crowned the Sole Survivor and will win $500 000!"

The first challenge was to build a shelter. Ravi led the construction, while Mia and Jace gathered materials. Ava designed the shelter, and Suyin ensured everyone stayed safe. By the end of the day, they had built a sturdy treehouse.

Next, they faced a food challenge. Lalita led the group to a grove filled with fruit trees, while Ava and Jace caught fish. Ravi and Suyin prepared a delicious feast, and Mia built a fire to cook the fish. They celebrated their success with a big dinner under the stars.

As the days went by, the challenges became tougher. They navigated dense forests, solved tricky puzzles, and faced their fears in dark caves. Each challenge tested their teamwork, courage and creativity.

One of the most exciting challenges was the Immunity Challenge. The castaways had to race through an obstacle course and retrieve a flag. Jace, with his quick reflexes, won the challenge and earned the immunity necklace.

The toughest part was the Tribal Council. Each week, the castaways had to vote off one of their own. It was always a difficult decision, but they stayed friends and supported each other.

In the end, it came down to Lalita and Mia. The final challenge was a test of endurance. They had to balance on a narrow beam over a pool of water. After a gruelling hour, Mia lost her balance, and Lalita was declared the Sole Survivor!

Mr Adventure presented Lalita with the grand prize of $500 000 and the title of Sole Survivor. The castaways cheered and celebrated their incredible journey. They had learned so much about themselves and each other, and they knew they would always be friends.

Grace Romano

Proper nouns are special names for people, places or things. Proper nouns always begin with capital letters. For example: *Queen Elizabeth, Australia, Anzac Day, Mazda*

1 Read the story "The young castaways". Complete the list of proper nouns from the text.

a A __________ I __________ **b** Y __________ S __________

c L __________ **d** M __________

e R __________ **f** S __________

g J __________ **h** A __________

i M __________ A __________ **j** S __________ S __________

k T __________ C __________

2 Categorise the proper nouns under the following headings.

People	Places	Titles

3 Match the common nouns in Box A with the proper nouns in Box B.

A

a politician __________ **b** explorers __________

c city __________ **d** author __________

e book __________ **f** river __________

g road __________ **h** sacred site __________

i planet __________ **j** aeroplane __________

k sportsperson __________ **l** company __________

B

i Nile
ii Main Street
iii Uluru
iv Julia Gillard
v *The Hobbit*
vi Microsoft
vii Beijing
viii Jupiter
ix Ash Barty
x Boeing 747
xi Shakespeare
xii Burke and Wills

Try it out!

On a separate piece of paper, use each of the letters of the alphabet to begin the **proper nouns** for names of:

a 26 countries **b** 26 girls' names **c** 26 boys' names **d** 26 animals.

(If you get stuck with the letter x, use it anywhere in your proper noun.)

Marina's open night

- a project called "Our heroes"
- sliced tomatoes
- 2 pianos
- 6 banjos
- bookshelves
- knives
- radios
- dictionaries
- a project on wolves
- live salmon and trout
- pet mice
- trousers with different kinds of stitches
- loaves of bread
- scissors
- stories
- sewing-needle boxes
- dolls' dresses
- autumn leaves
- street directories
- live goldfish
- Ari's project on butterflies
- models of teeth
- atlases of cities and countries
- Carla's project on monkeys
- Rema's project on mosquitoes
- a book called *Highways and Railways of Australia*
- videos of various class activities
- Anton's slide presentation on why wild dogs and dingoes are a threat to sheep and calves

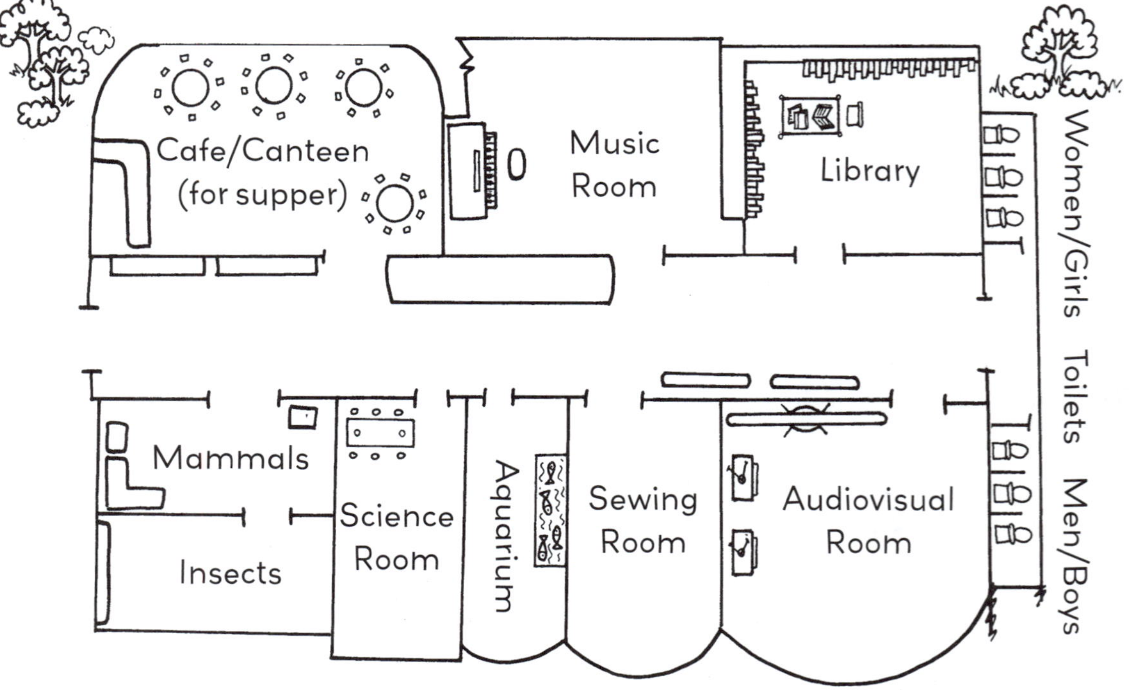

Do you know these rules for plural nouns?

1 For many nouns, just add *s* to make plural nouns. For example: *girls, lamps, books*
2 For nouns ending in *ch, sh, ss* or *x*, add *es*. For example: *matches, bushes, foxes*
3 For most nouns ending in *y*, change the *y* to *i* and then add *es*. For example: *cities, diaries*
4 For nouns ending in *y* following a vowel, just add *s*. For example: *boys, trays*
5 For most nouns ending in *f* or *fe*, change *f* or *fe* to *v* and then add *es*. For example: *halves, knives*
6 To form some noun plurals, there is a change in spelling. For example: *feet, children*
7 For most nouns ending in *o*, add *es*. For example: *potatoes, heroes*
8 For most nouns from other languages, and for nouns ending in *o* that have been abbreviated, just add *s*. For example: *pianos, kimonos, radios*

Did you know that some nouns exist only in plural form? For example, *scissors, binoculars, trousers*

1 Write the following nouns as plurals.

a woman ______ **b** calf ______ **c** key ______
d convoy ______ **e** room ______ **f** box ______
g wolf ______ **h** studio ______ **i** pliers ______
j shelf ______ **k** Saturday ______ **l** wallaby ______
m echo ______ **n** gas ______ **o** volcano ______
p X-ray ______ **q** photo ______ **r** banjo ______
s foot ______ **t** dictionary ______ **u** life ______

2 Change the following sentences to plural.

a The frightened donkey hid in the ditch as the wolf and the elf tramped by. ______

______

b Marni took her scissors, shears and needle and in a moment, she had created the most fantastic dress that the princess had ever seen. ______

______

3 Write plurals from the box to match these clues.

spies thieves brooches banjos mosquitoes aviaries attorneys cypresses

a blood-sucking insects ______ **b** lawyers ______
c secret agents ______ **d** musical instruments ______
e jewellery ______ **f** bird cages ______
g trees ______ **h** robbers ______

Try it out!

Look at the opposite page. Marina's school is holding an open night for parents. Marina has a box filled with things to display or use in the rooms and on the noticeboards. Help Marina get organised for the special night. On a separate piece of paper, write the name of each item in the best location possible. For example: *live goldfish – in the aquarium, street directories – in the library*

The loaded dog

Dave Reagan, Jim Bently and Andy Page were sinking a shaft at Stony Creek in search of a rich gold quartz reef which was supposed to exist in the vicinity.

They had a big, black, young retriever dog – or rather an overgrown pup, a big, foolish, four-footed mate, who was always slobbering round them and lashing their legs with his heavy tail that swung round like a stockwhip. Most of his head was usually a red, idiotic, slobbering grin of appreciation of his own silliness. He seemed to take life, the world, his two-legged mates, and his own instinct as a huge joke. He'd retrieve anything; he carted back most of the camp rubbish that Andy threw away. They had a cat that died in hot weather, and Andy threw it a good distance away in the scrub; and early one morning the dog found the cat, after it had been dead a week or so, and carried it back to camp, and laid it just inside the tent flaps, where it could best make its presence known when the mates should rise and begin to sniff suspiciously in the sickly, smothering atmosphere of the summer sunrise.

He used to retrieve them when they went in swimming; he'd jump in after them, and take their hands in his mouth, and try to swim out with them, and scratch their naked bodies with his paws. They loved him for his good-heartedness and his foolishness, but when they wished to enjoy a swim they had to tie him up in camp.

Henry Lawson

Adjectives are words that describe people, places, animals, things or ideas.
For example: *The* ***adventurous*** *trio was sinking a* ***deep*** *shaft in search of a* ***quartz*** *reef.*
Sometimes a writer adds more adjectives to sharpen the image for the reader.
For example: *a* ***rich gold quartz*** *reef*

Did you know that some common and proper nouns can be used as adjectives? For example: **birthday cake, boat refugee, Pacific gull**

1 Read the passage from "The loaded dog". Write eight adjectives that describe the men's dog.

____

____

2 Write adjectives from the passage that describe the following.

a the dog's tail ______________ **b** a joke ______________

c the dog's grin ______________ **d** the weather when the cat died ______________

e the atmosphere ______________

Adjectives are often used to compare things.
For example: *a big retriever; a bigger retriever; the biggest retriever*
a heavy tail; a heavier tail; the heaviest tail

3 Complete this table with suitable comparative adjectives.

large	larger	
fast		fastest
thick		
	naughtier	

Sometimes, instead of adding -er or -est when using comparative adjectives, we need to write *more* or *most* before them.
For example: *The dog was foolish. His dog was more foolish, but my dog was the most foolish.*

4 Use the adjectives in bold to compare three things.

a Zanetha was **excited**, Ella was ______________________ but Marli was ______________________.

b Dave was **suspicious**, Jarli was ______________________ but Antoni was ______________________.

5 Use adjectives from the box to complete these similes.

a as ______________ as a cucumber

b as ______________ as a lamb

c as ______________ as a fox

d as ______________ as an owl

gentle
cunning
wise
cool

A simile is a figure of speech that uses adjectives to compare things.
For example: *as slippery as an eel* (*slippery* is the adjective)

Try it out!

A sprinkling of **adjectives** can enliven writing, but be careful not to overdo it. On a separate piece of paper, use adjectives and interesting nouns to write a brief description of one of the following.

a a jungle scene **b** a desert landscape **c** a seashore on a stormy day

Rescue in downtown Pondsville

In downtown Pondsville, a peaceful day turned into chaos as a raging fire broke out in a tall building. Thick smoke billowed into the sky, and several people were trapped on the roof, desperately waiting for help.

Keen-eared Brave Bunny was the first to hear the emergency. Her sharp hearing and bravery made her sprint towards the scene. She contacted Dynamic Duck, known for his incredible speed and agility.

"Dynamic Duck, we need to act fast! People are trapped on the roof!" Brave Bunny exclaimed.

Dynamic Duck nodded and flapped his wings, ready to take action. "Let's gather the team!"

Next, they found Mighty Moose, whose immense strength was unmatched. "Mighty Moose, we need your help to clear the debris and create a safe path for the firefighters," Brave Bunny explained.

Mighty Moose nodded, his muscles rippling with determination. "Leave it to me!"

Meanwhile, Sky Glider, with her ability to glide and fly, joined the team. "I can help guide the people to safety from above," she offered.

As the friends arrived at the scene, they saw the flames growing fiercer. Dynamic Duck zoomed around the building, assessing the situation. "We need to get those people off the roof quickly!"

Brave Bunny used her keen hearing to locate the trapped individuals. "They're on the east side of the roof!" she shouted.

Mighty Moose charged through the burning debris, clearing a path for the firefighters. Sky Glider soared above, reassuring the trapped people that help was on the way.

Dynamic Duck, with his incredible speed, flew up to the roof and began guiding the people to the edge, where Sky Glider could help them glide down to safety. Brave Bunny stayed on the ground, coordinating with the firefighters who had just arrived – a brave team ready to extinguish the fire.

"Over here!" Brave Bunny called out to the firefighters. "We've cleared a path for you!"

The firefighters quickly set up their hoses and began battling the flames. With Mighty Moose's strength, they were able to move heavy obstacles out of the way, making their job easier.

Sky Glider and Dynamic Duck worked tirelessly to get everyone off the roof. One by one, the trapped individuals were safely brought down. The firefighters, with their expertise and bravery, managed to control and eventually extinguish the fire.

Grace Romano

An adjective tells us more about a noun. In sentences, an adjective usually comes before the noun it is describing. For example: *A **raging** fire broke out in a **tall** skyscraper.* (*fire* and *skyscraper* are nouns)
*Mighty Moose charged through the **burning** debris.*
*Sky Glider reassured the **trapped** people that help was on the way.*

1 Write the adjectives from the comic strip that are used in the following names.

a Bunny ______________________

b Duck ______________________

c Moose ______________________

2 Underline the adjectives that describe the nouns in each sentence.

a In downtown Pondsville, a peaceful day turned into chaos as a raging fire broke out in a tall skyscraper.

b Brave Bunny used her keen hearing to locate the trapped individuals.

c Dynamic Duck, known for his incredible speed and agility, flew up to the roof.

d Mighty Moose used his immense strength to clear debris, creating a safe path for the firefighters.

e Sky Glider soared above, guiding the trapped people to safety.

f The firefighters, a brave team, arrived and began battling the fierce flames.

Adjectives can have three degrees of comparison:

- positive – when the adjective is in its simplest form: **fast**, **ugly**, **dangerous**
- comparative – when the adjective compares two people, groups or things: **faster**, **uglier**, **more dangerous**
- superlative – when the adjective compares more than two people, groups or things: **fastest**, **ugliest**, **most dangerous**

Some adjectives compare. For example: *a **tall** building, a **taller** building, the **tallest** building*

3 Write adjectives of comparison in the gaps in these sentences. For example: *A hippopotamus is **larger** than a dog.*

a The people were brave, the animals were braver, but the firefighters were ____________ .

b Dynamic Duck's hearing is good, Mighty Moose's hearing is ______________ but Brave Bunny's hearing is ______________ .

c Locating the trapped people was difficult, clearing a path for the firefighters was ________ difficult, but getting everyone off the roof was the ________ difficult.

Try it out!

On a separate piece of paper, write three **adjectives** for each of the following.

a Dynamic Duck
b the people on the skyscraper
c the firefighters

Code Warriors: The Cyber Quest

Here are the main characters from the game Code Warriors: The Cyber Quest.

The cunning Harriet Hacker

The inventive and cybersafe Sam Spectra

The determined eco-warrior Jedda Jarra

The fast and agile Vani Valliant

The humorous and playful Naoki Nam

The irksome Troll

Jellybean

Sarah Haley

OXFORD UNIVERSITY PRESS

Adjectives are words that describe nouns.

For example: *a **soft, furry** toy. Biffo was the **funniest** clown at the circus.*

When adjectives or articles (*a*, *the*, *an*) are added to nouns, they form a noun group. Some adjectives can be formed by adding suffixes (endings) to nouns or verbs.

For example: *Count Meout is **detestable** = detest* (verb) + *-able*

Note: When adding endings to some words, the spelling of the base word must change before the ending is added. For example: *natur**e**, natur**al***

1 Use the suffixes in the box to change each noun or verb to an adjective.

-able -ous -ful -ing -ate -less -ive -al -ish -ant -ent -ic -ly

hack ______	invent ______	nature ______	humour ______
play ______	courage ______	protect ______	skill ______
environment ______	hero ______	danger ______	honour ______
fame ______	cheer ______	glamour ______	use ______
fashion ______	villain ______	objection ______	help ______
fool ______	rely ______	energy ______	fury ______
thought ______	disgrace ______	beauty ______	please ______
nerve ______	sheep ______	mind ______	consider ______
spite ______	monster ______	peace ______	faith ______
marvel ______	coward ______	fiend ______	care ______
self ______	chivalry ______	grace ______	style ______
affection ______	friend ______	child ______	power ______
fortune ______	agree ______	beast ______	ridicule ______

2 On a separate piece of paper, write noun groups by using the list of new adjectives you have written to expand the descriptions of the characters.

For example: *The highly inventive and cunning Harriet Hacker*
The skilful and protective Sam Spectra
The caring and considerate Jedda Jarra

Try it out!

How many **adjectives** can you form from the letters in the boxes below? You may use letters more than once.

S R E T I A H F N D Y U

My Australia

My Australia is
Walking through the streets of Punchbowl
With the smell of freshly roasted Lebanese
coffee kissing the Asian bakeries good morning
The eucalyptus towers overhead and the
frangipanis scent my breath
As we sing the unofficial national anthem
"I come from a land down under ..."
Living from beat to beat
Bumping down the streets
With Tupac on our tongues and
We're headed for the beach
Water so unapologetically salty to the eyes
But we take it in our stride
Remembering all the lessons at Greenacre pools
and at school
When Cronulla hit high tide

My Australia is barbecues
Or as my dad still says
Barr-be-ku
Meat sizzling on the fire
Homemade tabouli and tomato sauce
Pavlova cake and knafeh
The perfect cultural dichotomy
and it's not hard to see no matter
Our creed we always rep our team
Hashtag #WanderersFC

This country will never be tainted by cafe sieges
We will always ride together
From the mountains where the bushfires rage
we stand together
Down to the shore where the lifesavers age
Under that Great Southern Sun

My Australia is one
Where women wear their saris and their
colourful hijabs proudly
Men don sweat stained blue collars like war badges
You can get the best pho in Sydney
The realest Lebanese and Chinese
And you feel at ease because no one judges
your garlic breath or the parsley stuck in your teeth
It is finding the most authentic spices
In shops where signs in foreign languages
Sit like jewelled crowns atop their doors
It is neighbours passing handrolled food
over the fence
And always saying hello
It is all the stoic traditions
It is stoic – a community that has been hardened
by media headlines
It is targeted
It is judged
It is 3am sirens and perceived thugs

But it is also where the call to prayer
Gently interludes with the ringing
of church bells
It is co-existence
And artistic resistance
Like the 4elements Youth Hiphop Festival
And the largest poetry slam in the country

It is my Dad's voice 35 years on
Accent thick with resilience
Warm like an Autumn breeze
Smelling of petrol and truck smoke
and all the forgotten things
All the zaatar and the tahini and the crushed
petals that were once dreams
Saying
We are lucky
It's not perfect. But it's home.
It will never be perfect, but it will
always be home
My Australia is home.
When the rest of the world says no.

Sara Mansour

1 Find and write adjectives from the poem that best describe these nouns.

a coffee ______________________ b bakeries ______________________

c water ______________________ d meat ______________________

e sun ______________________

2 Find proper nouns in the poem to match these descriptions.

a The streets of which suburb ____________ b A famous rapper ____________

c Public pools ____________ d A football team ____________

e A beach ____________ f A type of cake ____________

3 Find noun groups in the story that build on these nouns.

a ____ coffee

b ____ spices

c ____ collars

d ____ traditions

4 Add a suffix to each of the following adjectives to form nouns.

For example: cool + *-ness* = coolness

a colourful ______________ b authentic ______________

c salty ______________ d judge ______________

5 Add a suffix to each of the following nouns to form adjectives.

a nation ______________ b home ______________

c tradition ______________ d culture ______________

Try it out!

Use **adjectives** to complete these sentences.

a The ______________ smell of freshly roasted Lebanese coffee kissed the ______________ Asian bakeries good morning.

b The ______________ eucalyptus towers overhead and the ______________ frangipanis scent my breath as we sing the unofficial national anthem.

Topic 1: Test your grammar

Nouns, adjectives and noun groups

1 Read the sentence below and shade the bubble next to the **common noun**.

Buster chased the ball across Royal Park.

a ◯ Buster b ◯ chased c ◯ ball d ◯ Royal Park

2 Read the sentence below and shade the bubble next to the **abstract nouns**.

Her bravery in overcoming her fear of heights inspired everyone around her.

a ◯ bravery b ◯ face c ◯ fear d ◯ everyone

3 Read the sentence below and shade the bubble next to the **collective noun**.

A large school of fish swam gracefully through the coral reef.

a ◯ large b ◯ school c ◯ fish d ◯ reef

4 Read the sentence below and shade the bubble next to the **abstract noun**.

Their friendship grew stronger over the years.

a ◯ friendship b ◯ grew c ◯ stronger d ◯ years

5 Shade the bubble below the **proper noun** in this sentence.

I would only get a game with the Bandits if I practised every day.

◯ ◯ ◯ ◯

6 Shade the bubble next to the correct **plural noun** for **dingo**.

◯ dingos ◯ dingi ◯ dingoes ◯ dingies

7 Shade the bubble next to the correct **plural noun** for **goose**.

◯ goose ◯ gooses ◯ goosies ◯ geese

8 Shade the bubble next to the **noun group** in this sentence.

We sailed quietly through the eerie fog.

◯ sailed quietly ◯ quietly through ◯ through the ◯ the eerie fog

9 Shade the bubble next to the **adjective** that best describes an ocean.

The ocean can be very ______ *during a storm.*

○ succulent ○ turbulent ○ wholesome ○ athletic

10 Shade the bubble next to the **adjective** that best describes a villain.

○ heroic ○ delicate ○ evil ○ homely

11 Shade the bubble next to the **adjective** that completes the following:

quick, ______ *, quickest*

○ quicker ○ quickly ○ quickening ○ quicks

12 Shade the bubble next to the **adjective** that completes the following:

bad, worse, ______

○ baddest ○ worser ○ worsest ○ worst

13 Shade the bubble next to the **comparative adjective** that would best complete this sentence.

Of all the dogs, he was the ______ *dog in the obedience class.*

○ smart ○ smarter ○ smartest ○ smarts

14 Shade the bubble next to the **comparative adjective** that would best complete this sentence.

I was good, he was ______ *but she was by far the best.*

○ gooder ○ better ○ bestest ○ goodest

How am I doing?

Tick the boxes if you understand.

I understand the difference between common, proper, collective and abstract nouns. ☐

I understand that there are different rules for making nouns plural. ☐

Adjectives describe nouns. ☐

I understand the difference between positive, comparative and superlative adjectives. ☐

Topic 2: Verbs, adverbs and prepositional phrases

Learning intention

We are learning to identify and use verbs, adverbs and prepositional phrases to make our writing more interesting and detailed.

Unit 2.1 Choosing verbs to sharpen ideas

James and the Giant Peach

And now the peach had broken out of the garden and was over the edge of the hill, rolling and bouncing down the steep slope at a terrific pace. Faster and faster and faster it went, and the crowds of people who were climbing up the hill suddenly caught sight of this terrible monster plunging down upon them and they screamed and scattered to right and left as it went hurtling by.

At the bottom of the hill it charged across the road, knocked over a telegraph pole and flattened two parked cars as it went by.

Then it rushed madly across about twenty fields, breaking down all the fences and hedges in its path. It went right through the middle of a herd of fine Jersey cows, and then through a flock of sheep, and then through a paddock full of horses, and then through a yard full of pigs, and soon the whole countryside was a seething mass of panic-stricken animals stampeding in all directions.

The peach was still going at a tremendous speed with no sign of slowing down, and about a mile farther on it came to a village.

Down the main street of the village it rolled, with people leaping frantically out of its path right and left, and at the end of the street it went crashing right through the wall of an enormous building and out the other side, leaving two gaping round holes in the brickwork.

Roald Dahl

Verbs tell us what is happening or being done. Talented authors, such as Roald Dahl, choose verbs carefully to create a sharper image for the audience. Look at the following example from the text on the opposite page. The author could have written: "animals *going* in all directions". Instead he wrote: "animals *stampeding* in all directions".

1 Read the extract from *James and the Giant Peach*. Circle the verbs that tell about the action of the peach.

A simple verb is usually one word that comes after the subject of the sentence.
For example: *The ball* ***bounced****. The children* ***ran****. James* ***climbed*** *the tree.*
Verbs answer questions such as: *What are you doing? What is it doing? What did they do? What will she do?*

2 Underline the simple verbs in these sentences.

a The peach rolled down the steep slope.
b The peach bounced down the steep slope.
c Faster and faster and faster it went.
d It charged across the road.
e They screamed.
f The peach flattened two parked cars.
g It came to a village.
h People leapt frantically out of its path.

A compound verb (verb group) can be two or more words that include a main verb and a helping verb. (The helping verb can also be called an auxiliary verb. An auxiliary verb helps identify the tense of the verb.)
The ball ***will bounce***. Here *bounce* is the main verb, *will* is the helping verb.
They ***are running*** *from the peach.* Here *running* is the main verb, *are* is the helping verb.

3 Underline the compound verbs (verb groups) in these sentences.

a The peach had broken out of the garden.
b Crowds of people were climbing up the hill.
c The monster was plunging down upon them.
d It went crashing right through the wall.
e The peach went rolling down the steep slope.
f The peach was still going.

4 Write the compound verbs from these sentences and then circle the auxiliary (helping) verbs.

a The workers were returning to the building site. ______________________
b The animals were stampeding in all directions. ______________________
c The peach had broken through the fence. ______________________
d James was waiting in the garden. ______________________
e Our hockey team is practising every day for the Grand Final. ______________________

Try it out!

On a separate piece of paper, write interesting sentences of your own using each of the **simple verbs** shown below as a **compound verb** (**verb group**).

a walk **b** fly **c** dance **d** bought **e** choose

The Tranquil Trekkers Club

May 2025

The Tranquil Trekkers Club Newsletter

Hi everyone and welcome to the May newsletter! It's mostly about rules this month, as the committee felt a few reminders might be in order.

First, some hiking rules …

Older members should always wear a white Tranquil Trekkers identity badge on hikes.

New members must wear their red Tranquil Trekkers identity badge on at least their first three hikes. This will certainly help our "Hiking buddy" system work better.

Now some club rule reminders …

- Meetings will take place on the first Saturday of each month.
- Could members please remember to bring a plate of food or a drink to each meeting?
- All members must remove their footwear before entering the new clubhouse.
- All members should use the rear door to enter the clubhouse. (The committee might relax this rule once the barbecue area is completed.)

General news

Congratulations to Emma, Max, Geti and Leo on their great hike to Mt Prospect and back – well done guys. We will post the photos on our site soon.

Remember that the general hike to Walpurra Bay will take place on Sunday 25 June (weather permitting) – all are welcome!

Any current members who would like to introduce new members to the club may do so at any monthly meeting. (We would welcome any new members.)

Finally, members, their friends and families can donate to the club online. If you would like to make a donation, talk to Sam or Mish. Any donation will be gratefully received.

See you all on Saturday 20 May. Don't forget to bring your wet weather gear – it's winter, remember!

Samantha Cerano (Club President)

Some verbs tell the degree to which something might happen. They tell us the level of certainty or probability of something happening.

These verbs are called modal verbs or modal auxiliaries. They are helping verbs and must always be used with a main verb. The 10 most common modal verbs are: *can, could, may, might, shall, should, will, would, must, ought to.*

1 Read the newsletter, then underline the modal verbs in these sentences. Remember, modal verbs can be more than one word.

a Meetings will take place on the first Saturday of the month.

b All members should use the rear door to enter the clubhouse.

c Members can donate to the club online.

d We will post the photos on our site soon.

e Older members should always wear a white Tranquil Trekkers identity badge on hikes.

f This will certainly help our "Hiking buddy" system work better.

g All members must remove their footwear before entering the new clubhouse.

2 Circle the modal auxiliary that correctly completes each of the following.

a Will / Shall you turn off the television?

b May / Can you ride a bicycle?

c Should / Shall they come back later?

d May / Will you open your books please?

3 Use a modal auxiliary from the information box at the top of the page to complete each sentence.

a ______________________ I please go to the toilet?

b ______________________ a fruit bat see in the dark?

c If I had the time I ______________________ play tennis with you.

d If you are not ready ______________________ I come back when you are?

Try it out!

Write four more rules for the Tranquil Trekkers Club. Include a **modal verb** in each rule.

____

____

____

____

The Amazing Verbo

The Amazing Verbo is standing.

The Amazing Verbo is waiting.

The drum is rolling.

The Amazing Verbo is growing tense.

The Flying Finns are jumping.

The time has come.

The Flying Finns are touching down.

The Amazing Verbo is flying.

The Amazing Verbo is soaring.

The Amazing Verbo is landing …

… badly.

Verbs can tell us when something has happened. Verbs tell us whether the action in a sentence is in the past, present or future. We call this verb tense.

For example: *I walked.* (past) *I am walking.* (present) *I will walk.* (future)
The bird flew. (past) *The bird is flying.* (present) *The bird will fly.* (future)

1 Write if these sentences are in the past, present or future tense.

- **a** The Flying Finns are jumping. ______
- **b** The time will come. ______
- **c** Yesterday I swam 12 lengths of the pool. ______
- **d** Now is the time to ask questions. ______
- **e** The cat crept slowly towards the bird. ______
- **f** On my sixteenth birthday I will be getting a motorbike. ______

2 Circle the correct past tense verb in each sentence.

- **a** Tezza has (broke/broken) another window with that cricket shot.
- **b** A burglar who forced the door open has (stole/stolen) the jewels.
- **c** I (saw/seen) what was happening.

3 Complete this verb tense table.

Verb	Past	Present	Future
write	have written or wrote	am writing *or* writes	will write
wear	______ or wore	______ or wears	______
know	have known or ______	______	______
______	have drunk or ______	are drinking or ______	______
sing	have sung or ______	______ or ______	______

4 Change the following sentences to the past tense.

For example: *On the camp we* ***will swim*** *for one hour every morning.*
On the camp we ***swam*** *for one hour every morning.*

- **a** I am flying to Brisbane tomorrow. ______
- **b** The farmer's paddock is full of corn. ______
- **c** Jedda is drinking her milk. ______

Try it out!

The story of the Amazing Verbo is written in the **present tense**. On a separate piece of paper, rewrite the story twice: once in the **past tense** and then again in the **future tense**.

There's something fishy going on

All fish are aquatic vertebrates, meaning they have a backbone and live in water. According to experts, there are approximately 24 000 species of fish in the world. Fish are an important source of food worldwide.

Oysters are marine molluscs. Oysters are unusual because they can be male one year and female the next!

Jellyfish have tentacles. The tentacles of the lion's mane jellyfish can reach up to 60 metres from its body. That's the length of two basketball courts. The collective noun for jellyfish is a **smack**.

Barracuda are saltwater fish. When hungry, a barracuda will hunt for a whole school of fish. When it has eaten its fill, the barracuda herds the remaining live fish into shallow water. It then keeps them prisoner by guarding them until it is ready to eat again at its leisure.

The largest fish of all is the whale shark, which can grow up to 15 metres long.

The electric eel is a freshwater predator. It has electric organs, which it uses to stun its prey. The electric eel can deliver a 500-volt shock. The usual power of a home's electricity supply is 240 volts!

The glassfish is completely transparent. All of its bones and organs can be clearly seen.

Some fish are actually known to get seasick!

Verbs can be doing verbs (e.g. *walked, ran, climbed*), saying verbs (e.g. *said, called, asked*), thinking verbs (e.g. *decide, consider, believe*), feeling verbs (e.g. *like, love, hate, wish*) or relating verbs (e.g. *am, is, are, was, were, has, have, had*). We often use relating verbs in the timeless present tense when we are stating facts such as the facts about fish on the opposite page. Timeless present tense is used to indicate actions that are always happening. For example: *All fish **are** aquatic vertebrates. Fish **live** in water. All fish **have** backbones.*

1 Underline the timeless present tense verbs in these sentences.

- **a** The whale shark is the largest fish of all.
- **b** Jellyfish live in smacks.
- **c** The glassfish is completely transparent.
- **d** Fish are an important source of food worldwide.
- **e** Jellyfish have tentacles.

Use the timeless present tense when:

- the action is general
- the action happens all the time
- the statement is always true.

2 Write timeless present tense verbs from the box to complete these sentences.

eat · live · is · have · are

- **a** Barracuda ________________ saltwater fish.
- **b** Omnivorous animals ________________ plants and meat.
- **c** Fish ________________ scales.
- **d** An oyster ________________ a marine mollusc.
- **e** All fish ________________ in water.

Try it out!

Write four or five facts about an animal that you know something about.
Make sure your facts are written in the **timeless present tense**.

Archie and Anna's exploration

Archie and Anna were exploring a mysterious cave on the beach. They eagerly entered the cave, their footsteps echoing loudly. The waves crashed rhythmically outside, creating a soothing background sound.

Archie led the way confidently, holding a flashlight that shone brightly. Anna followed, her eyes frequently scanning the walls. They moved cautiously, aware of the slippery rocks beneath their feet.

"Look at this!" Anna exclaimed excitedly, pointing to a shimmering pool of water. They knelt down and peered into the pool, where tiny fish swam gracefully.

They ventured deeper into the cave, the air growing cooler. Spotting a narrow passage, they immediately squeezed through it.

On the other side, they discovered a hidden chamber filled with sparkling crystals. The light from Archie's flashlight reflected off the crystals, illuminating the room beautifully.

"Wow, this is amazing!" Anna whispered softly. They explored the chamber thoroughly, marvelling at the natural beauty around them.

Getting hungry, they quickly retraced their steps, moving swiftly towards the entrance. They came out into the sunshine. "That was fantastic!" Archie said breathlessly. Their adventure had been thrilling, and they couldn't wait to share their story with their friends.

Grace Romano

Adverbs usually add meaning to verbs. They can tell us **how**, **when**, **where** and **how often**.

For example: *She walked quickly.* (How? *quickly*) *Let's go in now.* (When? *now*)
Put your boots there. (Where? *there*) *I have seen that film twice.* (How often? *twice*)

1 Write whether the adverbs in bold below tell **how**, **when**, **where** or **how often**.

a Archie led the way **confidently** ______

b Anna followed, her eyes **frequently** scanning the walls. ______

c The waves crashed rhythmically **outside** ______

2 Underline the adverbs in these sentences and write whether they are telling **how**, **when**, **where** or **how often**.

a They eagerly entered the cave, their footsteps echoing loudly. ______

b They ventured deeper into the cave, the air growing cooler. ______

c Spotting a narrow passage, they immediately squeezed through it. ______

Sometimes adverbs can be used to compare.

For example: *Archie ran quickly to the finish line. Anna ran more quickly, but Alex ran the most quickly of all.*

3 Use the above rules to help you complete this table of adverbs that compare.

Positive	Comparative	Superlative
bravely	more bravely	most bravely
powerfully		
helpfully		
fast		
late		
early		

Modal adverbs can be used with verbs to add a degree of certainty or possibility. For example: ***Perhaps** you forgot to pack your socks. It seemed **likely** he would miss the train. You **obviously** spent some of your pocket money. Perhaps, likely* and *obviously* are modal adverbs because they modify or tell us more about what is possible or certain. Modal adverbs can be more than one word. For example: *in fact, no doubt*

4 Circle the modal adverbs and underline the verbs they modify.

a His argument certainly convinced me.

b We absolutely loved the house.

c Sifan Hassan definitely won the race.

d The bus is probably running late.

Try it out!

On a separate piece of paper, write a new ending to the story, based on the sentence below. Use as many adverbs as possible.

Anna managed to grab a crystal as she rushed to the exit.

Wonder

I know I'm not an ordinary ten-year-old kid. I mean, sure, I do ordinary things. I eat ice cream. I ride my bike. I play ball. I have an XBox. Stuff like that makes me ordinary. I guess. And I feel ordinary. Inside. But I know ordinary kids don't make other ordinary kids run away screaming in playgrounds. I know ordinary kids don't get stared at wherever they go.

If I found a magic lamp and I could have one wish, I would wish that I had a normal face that no one ever noticed at all. I would wish that I could walk down the street without people seeing me and then doing that look-away thing. Here's what I think: the only reason I'm not ordinary is that no one else sees me that way.

But I'm kind of used to how I look by now. I know how to pretend I don't see the faces people make. We've all gotten pretty good at that sort of thing: me, Mom and Dad, Via. Actually, I take that back: Via's not so good at it. She can get really annoyed when people do something rude. Like, for instance, one time in the playground some older kids made some noises. I don't even know what the noises were exactly because I didn't hear them myself, but Via heard and she just started yelling at the kids. That's the way she is. I'm not that way.

Via doesn't see me as ordinary. She says she does, but if I were ordinary, she wouldn't feel like she needs to protect me as much. And Mom and Dad don't see me as ordinary, either. They see me as extraordinary. I think the only person in the world who realizes how ordinary I am is me.

My name is August, by the way. I won't describe what I look like. Whatever you're thinking, it's probably worse.

R. J. Palacio

Adverbs usually tell us more about verbs.
Adverbs that tell us how are called adverbs of **manner**.
For example: *I ate my ice cream quickly.* (How? *quickly*)
Adverbs that tell us when are called adverbs of **time**.
For example: *I played ball with my friends yesterday.* (When? *yesterday*)
Adverbs that tell us how often are called adverbs of **number**.
For example: *I wish that I could walk down the street just once without people looking away.* (How often? *once*)
Adverbs that tell us to what degree are called adverbs of **degree**.
For example: *She can get really annoyed when people do something rude.* (What degree? *really*)

1 Read "Wonder" and then circle the adverb in each of the following sentences and write the type of adverb. For example: *He fell (deeply) in love with the huntress.* (manner or degree)

a I ride my bike daily. ______

b I unexpectedly found a magic lamp. ______

c Once, in the playground, some older kids made some noises. ______

d I don't know what the noises were exactly. ______

e We've all gotten pretty good at that sort of thing. ______

Like some adjectives, some adverbs also compare.
For example: *I hit **hard**, he hits **harder** but she hits **hardest**.*
*The suitors ran **swiftly**. Melanion ran **more swiftly** but Atalanta ran the **most swiftly** of all.*

2 Complete this table of adverbs that compare.

Positive	Comparative	Superlative
swiftly	more swiftly	most swiftly
hard	harder	hardest
silently	more silently	
		most bravely
quickly		
wisely		

When we expand around a main adverb to add detail, this is sometimes called an adverb group.
For example: *more swiftly, extremely swiftly, so swiftly*

3 Use the adverb group *more swiftly* in a sentence of your own.

______

______

Try it out!

On a separate piece of paper, make a list of all of the **adverbs** you can find in "Wonder". When you have finished, compare your list with those of your classmates.

Tom Swifties

Come on through to my surgery.

Don't these lollies cost anything?

I'll change the globe for you.

What are you painting?

I think winter's nearly with us.

I took my raft over the river's rough water.

How far is it across the Nullarbor?

I like to sleep all the time when we go camping.

I wonder if the concrete's set yet.

What should I wear to my wedding?

Isn't that bag too heavy for me to lift?

Wouldn't you prefer a poodle?

You gave me two less than a dozen!

Oh no! Why didn't you water my plants while I was away?

What do we do after the high jump?

Next you move your counter up the ladder or down the snake.

I wonder when we'll be able to launch the boat.

Would you like me to get something for you?

I can see clearly through this window now.

I'm off to race in the Melbourne Cup.

Adverbs tell us more about verbs. Tom Swifties are a form of humorous word play. The words spoken by Tom Swift, an adventure hero, would be followed by an **adverb** that had something to do with what he had said. For example: *"I'm in bed with the measles," said Tom* ***infectiously***. (The word *infectiously* is an **adverb** meaning spreading germs or disease.)

1 Using the speech bubbles opposite, write what each of these "Tom Swifties" said.

a ______________________ asked Tom artfully.

b ______________________ said Tom, the builder, firmly.

c ______________________ said Tom, the cleaner, transparently.

d ______________________ said Tom tensely.

e ______________________ said Tam, the jockey, hoarsely.

f ______________________ said Tom intently.

g ______________________ asked Tom, the labourer, weakly.

h ______________________ thought Tom, the sailor, tidily.

i ______________________ said Tom, the adventurer, rapidly.

j ______________________ said Tom, the electrician, lightly.

k ______________________ asked Tom freely.

l ______________________ asked Tom eventually.

m ______________________ said Tom gamely.

n ______________________ asked Tom, the bridegroom, suitably.

o ______________________ asked Tom plainly.

p ______________________ asked Tom witheringly.

q ______________________ asked Tom doggedly.

r ______________________ said Dr Tom patiently.

s ______________________ asked Tom, the waiter, fetchingly.

t ______________________ said Tom, the weather forecaster, coldly.

Adverbs sometimes tell us more about adjectives. They are often used to downplay or add emphasis to an adjective. For example: *Tom Swifties are* ***very*** *funny*. (The adverb intensifies the adjective *funny*.)
Tom Swifties are ***somewhat*** *funny*. (The adverb tones down the adjective *funny*.)

2 Circle the **adverb** used to add emphasis to or downplay each bold adjective.

a I am extremely **upset** I won't see you.

b He was very **unhappy**.

c I am really **sorry** I missed you.

d She looked simply **uninterested**.

Try it out!

On a separate piece of paper, make up your own Tom Swifties using the **adverbs** below.

a fashionably **b** wickedly **c** colourfully **d** clearly

Mixed-up proverbs

When you read the proverbs below, you will notice that they have become jumbled. (See exercises on the opposite page.)

Birds in the hand flock together.

Never look a gift horse while the iron is hot.

A bird in glass houses is worth two before they're hatched.

Rome wasn't built over spilt milk.

Don't cross the bridge in a day.

Don't put all your eggs in the mouth.

Charity begins while the sun shines.

Strike at home.

Don't count your chickens in the bush.

People of a feather shouldn't throw stones.

Make hay until you come to it.

Don't cry in one basket.

A phrase is a group of words without a verb. A phrase sometimes does the work of an adjective to provide a fuller description. For example: *The girl* ***with red hair*** *...* *The shop* ***around the corner*** *...*
Prepositional phrases begin with prepositions such as *with, on, in, under, near, about, over, of, into, around.*

1 The proverbs on the opposite page are jumbled. Unjumble them and write them on a blank page in your workbook, so that they make sense. Now add prepositional phrases tocomplete these proverbs.

a Birds ______________________________ stick together.

b People ______________________________ should not throw stones.

c A bird ____________________ is worth two ____________________ .

2 Write the prepositional phrases from the box that best fit the characters below. Write roman numerals to match.

i	in a glamorous ball gown	**ii**	in oil-stained overalls	**iii**	with sore feet
iv	with a deep voice	**v**	with perfect balance	**vi**	in a camouflaged uniform
vii	with a weathered face	**viii**	with violin in hand		

a the opera singer ____________________ **b** the bushwalkers ____________________

c the acrobats ____________________ **d** the soldier ____________________

e the movie star ____________________ **f** the mechanic ____________________

g the farmer ____________________ **h** the musician ____________________

Prepositional phrases can also do the work of an adverb to tell **when**, **where** or **how** an action takes place.
For example: *She arrived* ***at six o'clock****.* (tells *when* she arrived)
The bus stopped ***by the school gate****.* (tells *where* the bus stopped)
The doctors worked ***with great skill****.* (tells *how* the doctors worked)

3 Underline the prepositional phrase from each sentence and write whether it is telling **when**, **where** or **how**.

a The exchange teacher comes from Brazil. ____________________

b The herd of elephants lumbered across the plain. ____________________

c Our school concert will begin at 7 o'clock. ____________________

d The waves crashed onto the rocks with a loud roar. ____________________

Try it out!

Write the **phrases** from the unscrambled proverbs that best tell us more about these words.

a built ____________________ **b** cry ____________________

c put (eggs) ____________________ **d** don't look (a gift horse) ____________________

The games we played

Below are five recollections by elderly people about the games they played when they were your age. Do you recognise any of the games? Remember that when these people were young, there were no computer games or electronic devices.

1 "We played a game called elastics. Two children would stand opposite each other with their legs apart and a long loop of sewing elastic around their ankles, creating a rectangular space. The others would jump in and out of the elastic without touching it. Sometimes, we would jump to a rhythm or rhyme. The elastic could be raised to the knees or higher, making the game more challenging and more fun. It could keep us entertained for hours. It was like a fast-paced variation of skipping."

2 "We played a card game called 'Fish'. Each player would get five cards, and the rest would form a draw pile. The goal was to collect sets of four cards of the same rank. On your turn, you would ask another player for a specific rank, such as 'Do you have any threes?' If they had any, they had to give them to you and you got another turn. If they didn't, they would say 'Go fish' and you had to draw a card from the pile. The game continued until all sets were collected. It was so much fun!"

3 "We played a game called hopscotch. We would draw a series of numbered squares on the ground with chalk.

Each player would take turns tossing a small object, like a stone, onto the squares in numerical order. Then, we would hop through the squares on one foot, skipping the square with the stone. If you stepped on a line or missed a square, you lost your turn. The goal was to complete the course and retrieve the stone without making any mistakes. It was a simple game, but we loved it."

4 "We played backyard cricket. We would set up a makeshift pitch in the backyard, using anything we could find for wickets, like bins or sticks. One player would bowl the ball, and the batter would try to hit it as far as possible. If the ball was caught or the wickets were hit, the batter was out. We took turns batting and bowling, and the game could go on for hours.

5 "We played a game called skipping. We would use a long rope, with one person at each end turning it. The rest of us would take turns jumping in and out of the rope, trying to keep up with the rhythm. Sometimes, we would chant rhymes or count how many jumps we could do without tripping. If you missed a jump or got tangled in the rope, you had to switch places with one of the turners. What a great way to keep us fit and healthy!"

Grace Romano

1 Find verbs in the recollections opposite that match the following definitions.

a To move quickly off the ground using your feet ______________________

b To inquire about something ______________________

c To throw something lightly ______________________

d To speak or sing rhythmically to music or a beat ______________________

e To create a mark on a surface ______________________

2 Write the past tense of these verbs. For example: *swim – swam*

a jump ______________________ **b** ask ______________________

c draw ______________________ **d** toss ______________________

e hop ______________________ **f** bowl ______________________

g chant ______________________ **h** skip ______________________

3 Underline or circle the adverb in each of these sentences.

a We happily played hopscotch for hours in the backyard.

b The children quickly jumped in and out of the elastics without touching them.

c During the game of Fish, she eagerly asked for more cards.

4 Add prepositional phrases to complete these sentences.

a We played elastics ______________________ .

b The children jumped in and out of the rope ______________________ .

c During the game of Fish, she asked for more cards ______________________ .

d We drew the hopscotch squares ______________________ .

e The batter hit the ball ______________________ .

Try it out!

Complete this table of **comparative adverbs**.

hard	harder	__________
well	__________	best
little	less	__________
__________	nearer	nearest
early	__________	earliest

Topic 2: Test your grammar

Verbs, adverbs and prepositional phrases

1 Shade the bubble below the **verb** in this sentence.

Several cars crashed on the busy freeway.

○ ○ ○ ○

2 Shade the bubble below the **simple verb** in this sentence.

The snake slithered silently towards the unsuspecting mouse.

○ ○ ○ ○

3 Shade the bubble next to the **compound verb** (verb group) in this sentence.

The passengers were waiting impatiently for the late train.

○ the passengers
○ waiting impatiently
○ were waiting
○ late train

4 Shade the bubble below the **auxiliary verb** in this sentence.

Police are looking for a man with a scar across his left cheek.

○ ○ ○ ○

5 Shade the bubble next to the **past tense verb** that completes this group, and then write the verb in the box.

[ ]*, is buying, will buy*

○ buys ○ buyed ○ bought ○ am buying

6 Shade the bubble below the **modal verb** in this sentence.

Fans should enter the stadium through the east gate.

○ ○ ○ ○

7 Shade the bubble next to the word that is *not* a **modal verb**.

○ might ○ would ○ will ○ run

8 Shade the bubble next to the sentence that is correctly written in the **past tense**.

○ Mitch has broken the light on his new bicycle.

○ Mitch has broke the light on his new bicycle.

○ Mitch has breaked the light on his new bicycle.

○ Mitch has broked the light on his new bicycle.

9 Shade the bubble that shows the following sentence written in the **past tense**.

During our English class we will write a story about a fearsome dragon.

○ During our English class we are writing a story about a fearsome dragon.

○ During our English class we writted a story about a fearsome dragon.

○ During our English class we wrote a story about a fearsome dragon.

○ During our English class we was writing a story about a fearsome dragon.

10 Shade the bubble below the **adverb** in this sentence.

The superhero used his powerfully built body to lift the stricken locomotive.

○ ○ ○ ○

11 Shade the bubble next to the **prepositional phrase** in this sentence.

Captain Spack Jarrow manoeuvred the boat alongside the jetty.

○ Captain Spack Jarrow

○ manoeuvred the boat

○ on the boat

○ alongside the jetty

How am I doing?

Tick the boxes if you understand.

Verbs tell us what is happening or being done in a sentence. ☐

Auxiliary verbs are helping verbs used with a main verb. ☐

Modal verbs tell how sure we are about taking an action. ☐

Adverbs add meaning to verbs telling when, where or how something happened. ☐

Prepositional phrases are small groups of words beginning with a preposition that add details about when, where, how and why. ☐

Topic 3: Text cohesion and language devices

Learning intention

We are learning to use a variety of cohesion and language devices to make our writing more interesting and descriptive.

Unit 3.1 Text cohesion – Antonyms, synonyms and homonyms

The fabulous Nym Brothers

Presenting those fabulous proponents of acrobatic dexterity …

What the critics said …

about
Syno Nym

Fantastic, wonderful, marvellous, amazing,
extraordinary, astonishing, incredible, stupendous!
Without a thesaurus what more can I say?

Theo Sawrus *(Sydney Mourning Harold)*

about
Anto Nym

Sometimes he's good and sometimes he's bad.
Sometimes he's happy but sometimes he's sad.
He rises to the ceiling then falls to the floor.
You'll be wishing for less rather than more.

Oppy Zit *(Melbourne Gerald Sunburn)*

about
Hommy Nym

A dear deer? Yes we saw that! A bare bear?
Yes we saw that too!

But what we really wanted to see was Hommy taking a trip on his trip across the tightrope. An acrobat all at sea – now that would have been something to see.

Pete Peat *(The Weekly Prophet – a non-profit magazine)*

Writers often **repeat key words** or **replace them** with synonyms or antonyms to add interest or compare and contrast a character's features.

Antonyms are opposites.
For example: *asleep/awake* *modern/ancient*

Synonyms are words with similar meanings.
For example: *big, large, huge, gigantic*

1 Match the words in the box with their antonyms.

strong minor down idle departure conclude

a up ______ **b** begin ______ **c** busy ______
d major ______ **e** weak ______ **f** arrival ______

Sometimes prefixes can be added to words to make antonyms.

2 Add the prefixes un-, dis-, mis-, in- or im- to form antonyms.

a behaviour ______ **b** activity ______
c accurate ______ **d** possible ______
e complete ______ **f** honest ______
g necessary ______ **h** usual ______

Sometimes suffixes can be changed to form antonyms. For example: *hopeful/hopeless*

3 Change the suffix of each word so that it becomes an antonym.

a careful ______ **b** useless ______
c cheerful ______ **d** merciful ______
e joyless ______ **f** pitiless ______

4 Circle the word that does not belong in each group of synonyms.

a fantastic wonderful marvellous ordinary amazing
b wobbly shaky steady rocky unsteady
c toss throw catch fling hurl
d strong weak powerful mighty sturdy
e halt cease stop commence conclude

Homonyms can be homophones or homographs. Homographs are words that are spelled the same but have different meanings. For example: **bow = ribbon, bow = front of a ship, bow = to bend at the waist, bow = a weapon for shooting arrows**
Homophones are words that sound the same but are spelled differently and have different meanings. For example: **blew, blue; wait, weight**

Try it out!

Write **homophones** and their meanings. For example: *dear = expensive* and *deer = a large mammal*

a boy = a young male and ______
b creek = a small stream and ______
c flower = a plant blossom and ______

A sting in the tail

The hobbit, Bilbo Baggins, has mysteriously lost his dwarf companions during the night. He finds himself alone in the silence and complete darkness.

That was one of his most miserable moments. But he soon made up his mind that it was no good trying to do anything till day came with some little light, and quite useless to go blundering about tiring himself out with no hope of any breakfast to revive him. So he sat himself down with his back to a tree, and not for the last time fell to thinking of his far-distant hobbit-hole with its beautiful pantries. He was deep in thoughts of bacon and eggs and toast and butter when he felt something touch him. Something like a strong sticky string was against his left hand, and when he tried to move he found that his legs were already wrapped in the same stuff, so that when he got up he fell over.

Then the great spider, who had been busy tying him up while he dozed, came from behind him and came at him. He could only see the thing's eyes, but he could feel its hairy legs as it struggled to wind its abominable threads round and round him. It was lucky that he had come to his senses in time. Soon he would not have been able to move at all. As it was, he had a desperate fight before he got free. He beat the creature off with his hands – it was trying to poison him to keep him quiet, as small spiders do to flies – until he remembered his sword and drew it out. Then the spider jumped back, and he had time to cut his legs loose. After that it was his turn to attack. The spider evidently was not used to things that carried such stings at their sides, or it would have hurried away quicker. Bilbo came at it before it could disappear and stuck it with his sword right in the eyes. Then it went mad and leaped and danced and flung out its legs in horrible jerks, until he killed it with another stroke; and then he fell down and remembered nothing more for a long while.

There was the usual dim grey light of the forest-day about him when he came to his senses. The spider lay dead beside him, and his sword-blade was stained black. Somehow the killing of the giant spider, all alone by himself in the dark without the help of the wizard or the dwarves or of anyone else, made a great difference to Mr Baggins. He felt a different person, and much fiercer and bolder in spite of an empty stomach, as he wiped his sword on the grass and put it back into its sheath.

"I will give you a name," he said to it, "and I shall call you Sting."

When writing, it is often necessary to **omit** or **replace words** to keep the text interesting.

For example: *Tina ate two bananas and Simon ate three bananas* would be better written as *Tina ate two bananas and Simon ate three.*

Another way a writer might keep text interesting for the reader is to repeat key words or replace them with pronouns or synonyms.

For example: *Bilbo was alone and miserable. The hobbit sat down and he pondered what he could do.*

In these sentences, *Bilbo* and *the hobbit* are interchangeable, while *he* is a pronoun replacing *Bilbo* and *the hobbit*.

1 Read "A sting in the tail", then rewrite the following sentences, **omitting** or **replacing words**, where necessary, to make the sentences easier to read.

a Bilbo took out his sword. He killed the spider with the sword.

____

b A strong sticky string was against his left hand. He found that his legs were bound with the strong sticky string. ______________________________

____

c He beat the creature off with his hands. The creature was trying to poison him.

____

2 Write the word that has been **omitted** or **replaced** by the word in **bold**.

a Bilbo dreamed of the delicious berries he had eaten that morning. Then he remembered he had **some** in his pocket. ______________________________

b "I have a powerful sword. Would you like **one**?" he said. ______________________________

3 Underline the words in the sentences below that have been used to **replace** the **bold** words.

a Sitting on the embankment was **a gnome**. The little fellow was wearing a yellow cap upon his head. In his left hand the odd chap held the lost map.

b **The grapes** hung in bunches from the vines. The fruit looked tender and juicy and we couldn't wait to pick and taste the delightful delicacies.

c **Roberto** strode into the garden. He was carrying **baby Sofia** on his shoulders and she had a huge grin across her face.

d I can't find **my umbrella**. Have you seen it?

e Congratulations to **Chloe**, **Lirah and Tan**. They achieved top marks in the spelling test. Well done all of you!

Try it out!

In the text on the opposite page, circle words that **replace** or refer to the main character. Use a different colour for each word replaced.

For example: *The **hobbit, Bilbo Baggins**, has mysteriously lost his dwarf companions during the night. He finds himself alone in the silence and complete darkness.*

Ivan goes for gold

It's the final night of weightlifting here at the Olympics. Heavyweight lifter Ivan de Golmeddle prepares for his final attempt. A successful lift for Ivan will mean GOLD! GOLD! GOLD!

Ivan approaches the barbell.

He bends and grasps the bar.

The photographers prepare themselves, for they are sure he will break the world record, which has stood for 20 years.

Ivan begins his lift.

He struggles.

He strains.

He puffs and pants.

But no world record or gold medal for Ivan today. However, we do believe that the photographers were very happy with their photos.

Pronouns or possessive pronouns can be used to replace or refer to a noun mentioned earlier in a sentence or text. Possessives answer the question: *Who owns it?* Possessives are: *my, yours, his, hers, its, ours* and *theirs*. For example: *That house belongs to* ***my*** *aunt. It is* ***hers***.

When we use a possessive with a noun, we call it a possessive adjective. For example: *her house, his knees*

1 Rewrite the sentences. Replace the repeated noun with a pronoun or possessive pronoun.

a Ivan wants the gold medal to be Ivan's. ______________________

b The photographers were very happy that the photos were the photographers'.

____

c Ivan struggles. Ivan strains. Ivan puffs and Ivan pants.

____

Personal pronouns refer to people or things: **I, me, we, us, you, he, him, she, her, it, they, them**

Possessive pronouns refer to ownership: **mine, ours, yours, his, hers, theirs**

First person pronouns are: *I, me, we, us, mine, ours*. They refer to those speaking (*me* or *us*). For example: *When* ***we*** *travelled to Mildura for a holiday* ***we*** *took* ***our*** *pets with* ***us***.

2 Use the first person pronouns and possessives to complete this description of the weightlifting contest written by Ivan de Golmeddle.

__________ approached the barbell. __________ bent __________ knees and grasped the bar which lay in front of __________ . __________ began to lift but __________ struggles were in vain. Unfortunately, the gold medal would not be __________ this year.

Second person pronouns are: *you* and *yours*. They refer to those spoken to (*you*).

For example: *Did* ***you*** *bring your homework today? Is that baseball bat* ***yours****?*

3 Change these sentences from first person to second person pronouns.

For example: *I was late for school. You were late for school.*

a I went on a holiday. ______________________

b Bree's room is much tidier than mine. ______________________

Third person pronouns are: *he, him, his, she, her, hers, it, its, they, them, theirs*. They refer to those spoken about (*him, her, it* or *them*). For example: ***He*** *will wear* ***his*** *raincoat while* ***he*** *waits for* ***them*** *to arrive.*

4 Rewrite the sentences in the third person.

a Last year I competed in my first Olympic Games. ______________________

____

b You couldn't lift your bar above your head. ______________________

____

Try it out!

In question 2, writing in the **first person** as Ivan de Golmeddle, you wrote about the weightlifting competition. On a separate piece of paper, complete the description from the photographers' point of view. Your description will be in the first person.

Did you hear about ...?

A

Did you hear about the skeleton that was attacked by a dog which ran off with some bones?

He didn't have a leg to stand on!

B

Did you hear about the man who made a hot dog stand by stealing its chair?

C

Did you hear about the jellybean that went to school to become a Smartie?

D

Did you hear about the restless medical student who couldn't become a doctor?

He didn't have the patients!

E

Did you hear about the one-handed man who was arrested trying to cross the road against the traffic lights?

He was on his way to the secondhand shop!

F

Did you hear about the wooden car that had wooden wheels and a wooden engine?

It wooden go!

G

Did you hear about my best friend who was sat on by an elephant?

Now he's my flatmate!

H

Did you hear about the tree whose leaves blushed every time they saw the nature strip?

Who, **which**, **whose**, **whom** and **that** are relative pronouns. Relative pronouns can stand in the place of a noun and can join two sentences.

For example: *Did you hear about the jellybean* ***that*** *went to school to become a Smartie?*
Did you hear about the jellybean? The jellybean went to school to become a Smartie.

1 Write the relative pronoun (or pronouns) from each joke on the opposite page.

a ______ **b** ______
c ______ **d** ______
e ______ **f** ______
g ______ **h** ______

2 Use a relative pronoun to join these sentences.

a Amanda turned 12 on Friday. Amanda is having a party on Saturday. ______

b This is the house. It was built by Mr and Mrs Rasheed. ______

c The athlete could not compete. Her ankle was injured. ______

d She is a reliable person. I can trust her. ______

Who refers only to people. For example: *Carrie,* ***who*** *is the school captain, thanked the visitors on our behalf.* **Which** refers to places, animals, things or ideas. For example: *The cat,* ***which*** *crossed the busy freeway, used up eight of its nine lives.* **That** refers to people, places, animals, things or ideas. For example: The cat that crossed the freeway was my friend's cat.

3 Write endings following the relative pronouns to complete these sentences.

a The soldier who ______
b The old oak tree, which ______
c The lady that ______

4 Which noun has been replaced by a relative pronoun? Circle it.

For example: *The footballer* ***who*** *broke his leg was out of action for 10 weeks.* (footballer leg weeks)

a I met a boy called Anthony **whose** mother drives a truck. (boy mother truck)
b On the tractor is the farmer **who** killed the deadly snake. (tractor farmer snake)
c The bank was robbed by a criminal **that** wore a gorilla mask. (bank criminal mask)

Try it out!

On a separate piece of paper, write your own sentences containing these **relative pronouns**:

who *which* *whose* *that*

Unit 3.5 Text cohesion – Paragraphs, topic sentences and text connectives

Why the Moon waxes and wanes

Myths and legends were used by cultures in the past to explain why things are the way they are. Here is a legend from the Iroquoian people of North America to explain, in their beliefs, why the Moon changes its shape during the course of a month.

Once, according to legend, the Sun and the Moon were husband and wife. They lived together side by side, travelling across the sky. **Each day** they would reach the hole at the edge of the sky, and the Sun, being the more important, would pass through, followed by the Moon.

One day, the Moon quarrelled with the Sun. She pushed through the hole at the edge of the sky before her husband. This action enraged the Sun. He scolded his wife, the Moon, and sent her away to the dark world below.

Great Turtle, the master of all animals, heard of the argument between the Sun and the Moon. He set off to search for the Moon and eventually found her pining away. She had lost most of her light and was so thin that instead of a ball she was merely a tiny crescent.

The Great Turtle spent much time with the Moon. He coaxed and cajoled and mended her broken heart and set her on her own course again. **Gradually** she became her own round self once more and she travelled across the sky in search of her husband.

However, the Sun refused to recognise his wife and as she approached he turned away from her. The Moon began to pine away again.

And so the cycle continues to this day. The Moon grows bright and radiant with hope, only to be ignored by her husband. Slowly she pines away, shrinking with sorrow as she follows the unforgiving Sun across the sky.

adapted from an Iroquoian legend

Paragraphs are used to organise information into logical sections so that the text is more easily understood. Paragraphs usually contain a number of sentences about one particular point. A topic sentence often begins a paragraph. It introduces or summarises the main point of the paragraph.

The *first paragraph* in a text body is often an introductory paragraph. It introduces us to what the text is about. The *final paragraph* in a text body is usually a concluding paragraph. It sums up what the text has been about. The *first word of a paragraph* is usually indented or written further in from the margin than the rest of the paragraph.

1 Read "Why the Moon waxes and wanes", then answer the questions below about the paragraphs and topic sentences in the story.

- **a** How many paragraphs does the story have? ____________________
- **b** Write the first sentence of the introductory paragraph. ____________________
____
- **c** Write the first sentence of the concluding paragraph. ____________________
____
- **d** How many sentences are there in the fourth paragraph? ____________________
- **e** Which paragraph introduces the Great Turtle? ____________________
- **f** Which paragraph tells us how the Sun reacted to the Moon's rudeness? ____________________
- **g** Write the topic sentence the author has used in the third paragraph. ____________________
____

Text connectives help to link text together. They give the reader signs about what is likely to come in the text.

2 Copy the six text connectives that the author has used in the story.

____

____

Try it out!

On a separate piece of paper, write five to 10 **paragraphs** about one of the topics below. Remember to include an introductory paragraph and a concluding paragraph. Your paragraphs can be any length. Begin each paragraphs with a **topic sentence** and, wherever possible, use **text connectives** of your own or from the box below.

- Why the Moon waxes and wanes
- A report about some recent sports results
- How the echidna got her spines
- My hobby
- Explain how to care for a pet (of your choice)
- Why the tiger has stripes
- The best day of my life so far
- Skateboards, bikes, skates and scooters!
- My typical day
- How the mountains and rivers were formed

Text connectives: *for example, in other words, therefore, so, then, next, afterwards, soon, finally, later, firstly, also, furthermore, otherwise, however, besides, even so, despite this, though*

Simmo and Lee's team of the century

Sports broadcasters Simmo and Lee have finally decided on the six players that will make up their TEAM OF THE CENTURY.

Fullback: Orson Carte

Orson Carte

Simmo says … Orson is as old as the hills, and he's as safe as a bank in defence. He's as strong as an ox, as hard as nails and as cool as a cucumber in a crisis. Attacks find it difficult to get past him because he is like a rock on that fullback line.

Halfbacks: Amanda Lynne and Owen Ulotts

Amanda Lynne

Lee says … Young Mandy is as brave as a lion and as swift as an arrow. She is as light as a feather and moves like a ballerina. She is also as tough as old boots.

My choice for the other halfback is Owen Ulotts, who can run like the wind and can go through packs like a steam train.

Owen Ulotts Carte

Centre: Bootsun Hall

Simmo says … You can't really go past the veteran Bootsun in this position. Built like a tank, as fit as a fiddle, as graceful as a swan and always as busy as a bee. What more could you ask for?

Bootsun Hall

Forwards: Willy Kickett and Rhoda Tramm

Lee says … Willy moves like a cat. He's as sly as a fox and has the eye of a hawk.

Willy Kickett

Simmo says … Rhoda will be a good back-up for Willy. She is as agile as a monkey, she attacks the ball like a demon and then strikes like lightning – I think she'll have a top game.

Here's what **Coach Tom Artow** had to say about his team: This team is like a machine – they're like clockwork. When they train they are as keen as mustard and, come game day, I think, as a unit, they'll be as sharp as a tack. I'll be as proud as a peacock if they win on Saturday.

Simmo's tip for Saturday: The Team of the Century by 100 points or I'm as silly as a sausage.

Lee's tip for Saturday: The Team of the Century by 50 points or I'm as foolish as a court jester.

Rhoda Tramm

A simile is used to compare one thing with another. A simile tells us that something is *like* something else. Similes begin with *like* or *as*.

For example: *The moon was **like** a grapefruit.*
*The water of the lake was **as** clear as crystal.*

1 Write two similes that have been used to describe each character.

a Orson Carte ______
b Amanda Lynne ______
c Bootsun Hall ______
d Willy Kickett ______
e Rhoda Tramm ______

Remember: You can make your writing more lively by using similes. But don't overdo it in the way that Simmo and Lee have done on the opposite page.

2 Write the names of the characters who have been compared using similes.

a a steam train's power ______
b a swan's grace ______
c an ox's strength ______
d a monkey's agility ______
e a peacock's pride ______
f an arrow's speed ______
g a hawk's vision ______
h a jester's silliness ______

3 Complete the following similes using words from the box.

toast, eel, sin, owl, egg, daisy, pancake, mouse, feather, bat, dog, lamb

a as wise as an ______
b as fresh as a ______
c as bald as an ______
d as blind as a ______
e as ugly as ______
f as flat as a ______
g as light as a ______
h as gentle as a ______
i as sick as a ______
j as warm as ______
k as slippery as an ______
l as quiet as a ______

4 Use words from the box to complete these similes.

playful, blanket, gold, jelly, dungeon, snow

a Snow covered the ground like a ______.
b He was as ______ as a kitten.
c The fleece on Mary's lamb was as white as ______.
d The hallway was as dark as a ______.
e The children were rewarded for being as good as ______.
f Before her concert performance, Mamie's legs were like ______.

Try it out!

On a separate piece of paper, make up your own **similes** by completing the following.

a as ... as silk
b her knees were like ...
c as nervous as ...
d as pretty as ...
e he ran like ...
f it sank like ...
g as sharp as ...
h he crashed like ...

Meet a metaphor

Rod was forced to eat his words.

Cassie is full of beans today.

Mark Diswright was over the moon with his test results.

Jenny is the apple of her Granny's eye.

Myra's legs turned to jelly at the sight of the huge audience.

It was raining cats and dogs.

We use metaphors to make our writing more colourful. Like a simile (see Unit 3.6), a metaphor is a word picture. It compares something or someone to something as if it were that thing.

For example: *the night was a cloak*
she played second fiddle
the Moon was a grapefruit

A simile compares one thing to another: **He was as cold as ice.**
A metaphor uses words to say that two things are the same: **His hands were icicles.**

1 Match the metaphors on the opposite page with their meanings below.

a very happy and excited ______

b lots of energy ______

c regret what has been said ______

d to be adored by someone ______

e raining very heavily ______

f in a very nervous state ______

2 Underline and then write your own explanations for the metaphors used in the sentences below.

a During the search for the missing dog, he was a tower of strength to the family.

______

b When it comes to the garden, Aunty Em certainly has green fingers. ______

______

c A way to recycle old tyres? Now there's food for thought. ______

______

d Poor Tim has another broken heart. ______

e During the closing stages of the game, Terri was a tiger in the packs. ______

______

f "We will leave no stone unturned in our search for the culprits," said Sergeant Clark.

______

Try it out!

On a separate piece of paper, explain what you think these **metaphors** mean.

a Her blood froze. **b** He waited with his heart in his mouth.

c She is a live wire. **d** They were down in the dumps. **e** His blood boiled.

Unit 3.8 Extension – Text cohesion and language devices

Celebrations

Eid al-Fitr

During the holy month of Ramadan, those of Muslim faith do not eat or drink between sunrise and sunset. Fasting during Ramadan demonstrates to Muslims that the good things in life should not be taken for granted. It is also a reminder that the poor and destitute of the world suffer from constant hunger.

Eid al-Fitr celebrates the end of the Ramadan fasting period. The word **eid al-fitr** is an Arabic word which means "breaking the fast". For three days Muslims celebrate a joyous festival of feasting, visiting loved ones and exchanging gifts.

Trung Thu

Trung Thu is a Vietnamese celebration held on the 15th day of the eighth lunar month. The festival celebrates the beauty of the Moon. During the Trung Thu, families gather together and children are spoilt with treats and tasty moon cakes, which are traditional sweet-filled cakes. Children will often wear colourful masks and carry glowing lanterns, which represent the Moon, out into the streets.

Hannukah

Hannukah is a Jewish festival – a festival of lights. It is celebrated for eight days, throughout which a candle on a **menorah** (candelabra) is lit each evening. During Hannukah, children receive a small present each evening. Special food such as **latkes** (potato cakes) are eaten during Hannukah.

Holi

Holi is a springtime Hindu festival celebrated in March by Hindus around the world. Holi coincides with the harvesting of wheat in India. On the evening before Holi, people light large bonfires to drive away evil spirits. On the following morning, people cover themselves with coloured powders and then squirt water over each other, covering themselves in a colourful mess. Children love Holi because it is a time when they are allowed to be as messy as they like.

Chinese New Year

Chinese New Year is one of the world's most colourful celebrations. Chinese New Year begins on the first day of the Chinese calendar, which is usually in February. The festival lasts for 15 days and it is said that good luck, happiness and wealth for the new year will come to those who celebrate during this time. It is a time for feasting, colourful processions and family get-togethers. On New Year's morning children are given "lucky" money in red envelopes.

1 Find **antonyms** in "Celebrations" for these words.

a sunrise ______________________ **b** rich ______________________

c ugliness ______________________ **d** good ______________________

e tidy ______________________ **f** sadness ______________________

2 Draw lines to match the words in Box A with their **synonyms** in Box B.

A	B
sunset	needy
poor	vibrant
celebrate	dusk
traditional	happy
joyous	commemorate
colourful	customary

3 Draw a circle around the correct **homonyms** in theses sentences.

a We sometimes **need/knead** to be reminded that **their/there** are **poor/pour** people in our world.

b **Your/You're allowed/aloud** to be messy during the celebration of Holi.

c **Its/It's** Trung Thu so **its/it's** time for delicious **sweet/suite** treats.

4 Complete these sentences using **possessive pronouns** to fill the gaps.

a Ravi covered ______________ face with coloured powder and then began squirting ______________ friends with water.

b "______________ mask is made of card," said Minh, "but ______________ is made of crepe paper."

c Isabel's mother brought out ______________ latkes and placed them in the middle of ______________ table.

Try it out!

Complete these **similes** and **metaphors**.

a as quick as ______________________ **b** as hungry as ______________________

c as strong as ______________________ **d** as happy as ______________________

e the Moon was a ______________________

f the waves crashed to the shore like ______________________

Topic 3: Test your grammar

Text cohesion and language devices

1 Shade the bubble next to the **antonym** for **busy**.

- ◯ idle
- ◯ busily
- ◯ unbusy
- ◯ business

2 Shade the bubble next to a **synonym** for **dreadful**.

- ◯ dreadless
- ◯ wonderful
- ◯ awful
- ◯ pleasant

3 Shade the bubble next to a **prefix** that could be used to make **patient** an antonym.

- ◯ im-
- ◯ un-
- ◯ in-
- ◯ mis-

4 Shade the bubble next to a **suffix** that could be used to change **merciful** to an antonym.

- ◯ -tion
- ◯ -less
- ◯ -able
- ◯ -ment

5 Shade the bubble next to the **possessive pronoun** that would complete this sentence.

The travellers waited with [ ] *bags inside the airport terminal.*

- ◯ there
- ◯ their
- ◯ they
- ◯ they're

6 Shade the bubble that shows which point of view the following sentence is written in.

I waited patiently until it was my turn and then I started my performance.

- ◯ first person
- ◯ second person
- ◯ third person
- ◯ fourth person

7 Shade the bubble that shows which point of view the following sentence is written in.

Later today they will arrive on their bikes at the rendezvous point.

- ◯ first person
- ◯ second person
- ◯ third person
- ◯ fourth person

8 Shade the bubble next to the **possessive pronoun** that would complete this sentence.

Monti put on [ ] *slippers and relaxed in* [ ] *favourite chair.*

- ◯ he
- ◯ him
- ◯ he's
- ◯ his

9 Shade the bubble below the **relative pronoun** in this sentence.

The man, who limped badly, struggled to get off the tram.

○ ○ ○ ○

10 Shade the bubble below the **text connective** in these sentences.

Preheat your oven to 180°C. Next, prepare your vegetables.

○ ○ ○ ○

11 Shade the bubble next to the word that would best complete this **simile**.

As straight as an [ ]

○ highway ○ barrel ○ egg ○ arrow

12 Underline the three **metaphors** that have been used in this verse from a well-known poem.

The wind was a torrent of darkness among the gusty trees,
The moon was a ghostly galleon tossed upon cloudy seas.
The road was a ribbon of moonlight over the purple moor,
And the highwayman came riding up to the old inn door.

How am I doing?

Tick the boxes if you understand.

Antonyms are opposites. ☐

Synonyms are words with similar meanings. ☐

Homonyms are words that look or sound the same. ☐

Possessive pronouns refer to ownership. ☐

Relative pronouns such as *who*, *which*, *whose*, *whom* and *that* can stand in the place of a noun OR join two sentences. ☐

Similes and metaphors are language devices that make our writing more descriptive and entertaining. ☐

Topic 4: Sentences, clauses, conjunctions, direct and indirect speech and apostrophes

Learning intention

We are learning to write a variety of sentences and use correct punctuation for different purposes.

Unit 4.1 Simple sentences – One main clause

I beg your pardon!

The politician was being cooked on the stove.

The smelly sock outsmarted the farmer.

My little brother was elected Prime Minister.

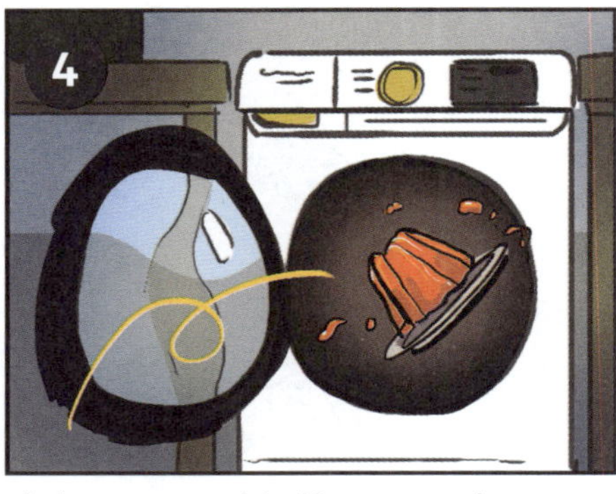

A huge red jelly was thrown into the washing machine.

The monster tickled the dog's belly.

The fox wobbled about on my plate.

My breakfast gobbled up the dwarves.

Simple sentences are made up of one main clause that can usually be divided into two parts:

a what is being talked about in the sentence (the subject) and

b what the rest of the sentence says about it (the predicate). The predicate always begins with a verb.

For example: *The cat meowed for its milk.* What is being talked about? *The cat* (subject)
What are we saying about it? That it *meowed for its milk.* (predicate)

1 On the opposite page, the subjects and predicates have been mismatched to make silly sentences. Rewrite the sentences correctly and then underline the subject in red and the verb that introduces the predicate in blue or black.

a ____________________

b ____________________

c ____________________

d ____________________

e ____________________

f ____________________

g ____________________

2 Write down the subject in each of these sentences.

a The audience clapped enthusiastically. ____________________

b The acrobat flipped casually over the barrel. ____________________

c Everyone at the party had a really great time. ____________________

3 Underline the predicates in these sentences.

a The jockey fell heavily.

b Our neighbour won the lottery.

c Smidge barked loudly at the intruder.

4 Circle the correct verb that agrees with the bold subject.

a **We** (go/goes) to the movies every month.

b The **silly sentences** (was/were) quite funny.

Remember, the subject and verb in a clause or simple sentence must be in agreement.

Try it out!

On a separate piece of paper, use the mixed-up sentences and **predicates** on the opposite page to write four of your own silly sentences. Make sure the **subject** and **verb** are in **agreement**.

For example: *The smelly sock was elected Prime Minister.*

You might also like to illustrate your sentences.

Transport quiz

Subjects		
	Spacecrafts	
Container ships	A tanker	Ferries
Locomotives	A Formula One car	Catamarans
A cruise ship	Hovercrafts	A prime mover
A skidoo	A turbojet	Tandems

Verbs and objects		
transports oil or other liquids	flies long distances carrying passengers	transport people, cars and trucks
use air cushions on land or water	carry two people	carries people on ocean-going leisure trips
races around tracks	hauls a trailer	sail on two or more hulls
carry containers	fly into space	tow freight cars
		slides across snow

The subject and verb of a sentence must agree in number. If the subject is singular, then the verb must be singular. For example: *The box* ***is*** *empty.* If the subject is plural then the verb must also be plural. For example: *The boxes* ***are*** *empty.*

1 Complete the transport quiz opposite by matching the subjects to the correct verbs and objects.

For example: *Container ships carry containers.*

a A tanker ______________________________.

b Locomotives ______________________________.

c Ferries ______________________________.

d A Formula One car ______________________________.

e A turbojet ______________________________.

f A skidoo ______________________________.

g Spacecrafts ______________________________.

h Catamarans ______________________________.

i A cruise ship ______________________________.

j Hovercrafts ______________________________.

k Tandems ______________________________.

l A prime mover ______________________________.

When collective nouns, money, lengths, weights and time are the subject of a sentence, they always take a singular verb in order to agree. For example: *A flock of birds* ***is*** *in the treetops.*

2 Circle the verb that agrees with the subject.

a Seventy-five cents (was/were) all that she had left.

b My team (is/are) winning by three goals.

c The crowd (surge/surges) forwards.

Some words that end in *s* are really singular. For example: ***Measles*** **is causing havoc at the school.**

Words such as *everybody, anybody, nobody, each, either* and *neither* always take a singular verb in order to agree. For example: *Either Mick or Sally* ***is*** *to blame.* *Everybody* ***was*** *waiting for Mr Toms to arrive.*

3 Circle the verb that agrees with the subject.

a Everybody (was/were) wearing sunhats.

b Neither of the sisters (are/is) at school today.

c Each suspect (was/were) thoroughly searched by the police at the airport.

Try it out!

Write the **verb** *is* or *are* following these **subjects**.

a the choir ________ **b** the pair of trousers ________ **c** the police ________ **d** the cattle ________ **e** the crew ________

Unit 4.3 Subject–verb–object–phrase

Whacky sentences

Subjects

The Prime Minister ...

The wombat ...

The weird alien ...

My teacher ...

The scary monster ...

The hairy puppy ...

The farmer ...

The children ...

Verbs

... met ...

... ate ...

... attacked ...

... taught ...

... chased ...

... licked ...

... milked ...

... loved ...

Objects

... the Queen ...

... a soggy pickle sandwich ...

... the prickly cactus ...

... the littlies ...

... my irritating brother ...

... a plate of smelly cream ...

... a green spotted cow ...

... the funny clown ...

Phrases

... at the Grand Prix

... on the rubbish tip

... in the desert

... every Monday morning

... in front of the shed

... under the table

... in the back paddock

... with the baggy pants

On the opposite page, you can see different sentence parts that make up a **main clause**. The subject tells us who or what the sentence is mainly about. The verb tells us what action the subject is carrying out. The object is the person or thing in the sentence that is having something done to them. Phrases add details about where, when, how or why.

For example:	*My teacher*	*teaches*	*the littlies*	*every Monday morning.*
	subject	**verb**	**object**	**phrase**

1 If you read each part of the sentences on the opposite page in the order in which they are written, they will make sense. However, if you mix and match the different parts of the sentences, they will become very interesting. Write six new sentences by mixing the sentence parts.

For example: *The Prime Minister attacked a soggy pickle sandwich in front of the shed.*

____

____

____

____

____

____

2 Write the subjects in these simple sentences (main clauses).

a The dog barked at the stranger with the dark glasses. ______________

b The old woman stirred the pot while chanting softly. ______________

c Jeda Jones threw a stick at the thieving crows. ______________

3 Write the objects in these simple sentences (main clauses).

a Mr Lu carried Simon to the waiting ambulance. ______________

b The pirates found their treasure in a cave on a deserted island. ______________

c Julius Caesar commanded a legion in Ancient Rome. ______________

4 Underline the phrases in these simple sentences (main clauses).

a He chased me from the ship.

b The horse pulled the cart over the bridge.

c On the starboard side of the ship, the sailors raised the anchor.

5 Write the nine verbs that have been used in the sentences in questions 2, 3 and 4.

____

____

Try it out!

On a separate piece of paper, write one **sentence** about each of the topics listed below, making sure that each sentence contains a **subject**, a **verb**, an **object** and a **phrase**.

a a passage of play in a game **b** a description of a wintry day **c** your favourite day of the week

Mongoose

He was a mongoose, rather like a little cat in his fur and his tail, but quite like a weasel in his head and his habits. His eyes and the end of his restless nose were pink; he could scratch himself anywhere he pleased, with any leg, front or back, that he chose to use; he could fluff up his tail till it looked like a bottle-brush, and his war-cry, as he scuttled through the long grass, was: "Rikk-tikk-tikki-tikki-tchk!"

One day, a high summer flood washed him out of the burrow where he lived with his father and mother, and carried him down a roadside ditch. He found a little wisp of grass floating there, and clung to it till he lost his senses. When he revived, he was lying in the hot sun on the middle of a garden path, very draggled indeed, and a small boy was saying: "Here's a dead mongoose. Let's have a funeral."

"No," said his mother; "let's take him in and dry him. Perhaps he isn't really dead."

They took him into the house, and a big man picked him up between his finger and thumb, and said he was not dead but half choked; so they wrapped him in cotton-wool, and warmed him, and he opened his eyes and sneezed.

"Now," said the big man (he was an Englishman who had just moved into the bungalow); "don't frighten him, and we'll see what he'll do."

It is the hardest thing in the world to frighten a mongoose, because he is eaten up from nose to tail with curiosity. The motto of all the mongoose family is, "Run and find out," and Rikki-tikki was a true mongoose. He looked at the cotton-wool, decided that it was not good to eat, ran all round the table, sat up and put his fur in order, scratched himself, and jumped on the small boy's shoulder.

"Don't be frightened, Teddy," said his father. "That's his way of making friends."

"Ouch! He's tickling under my chin," said Teddy.

Rikki-tikki looked down between the boy's collar and neck, snuffed at his ear, and climbed down to the floor, where he sat rubbing his nose.

"Good gracious," said Teddy's mother, "and that's a wild creature! I suppose he's so tame because we've been kind to him."

"All mongooses are like that," said her husband. "If Teddy doesn't pick him up by the tail, or try to put him in a cage, he'll run in and out of the house all day long. Let's give him something to eat."

from *Rikki-Tikki-Tavi* by Rudyard Kipling

Coordinating conjunctions are joining words used mainly to join two main clauses or simple sentences of equal importance. The main coordinating conjunctions are *and, but, so* and *or.*

For example: *He sat up* ***and*** *put his fur in order.*
(*and* joins the equally important sentences *He sat up.* and *He put his fur in order.*)

Coordinating conjunctions can also be used to join two matching language features.

For example: *The mongoose's fur* ***and*** *tail were like a cat's.* (*and* joins the nouns *fur* and *tail*)
A high summer flood washed him out of the burrow ***and*** *down a roadside ditch.*
(*and* joins the phrases *out of the burrow* and *down a roadside ditch*)

1 Use the clues to help you underline the coordinating conjunctions in each sentence.

a He could scratch himself with any leg, front or back. *(I connect two adjectives.)*

b Rikki ran around the table and onto the boy's shoulder. *(I connect phrases.)*

c The mongoose lived with his mother and father. *(I connect two nouns.)*

d Rikki was a little like a cat in his fur and his tail but he was like a weasel in his head and habits. *(I connect two noun groups. I connect two main clauses. I connect two nouns.)*

Subordinating conjunctions join main clauses with subordinate clauses. Some common subordinating conjunctions are *because, if, after, although, until/till, since, where, when, while* and *as.*

Subordinate clauses start with a subordinating conjunction and cannot stand alone.

For example, the subordinate clause *because Jane rang the bell* needs a main clause before it can be used.

The children assembled at the classroom door **because Jane rang the bell**.

main clause: *The children assembled at the classroom door*
subordinate clause (dependent clause): **because Jane rang the bell**

2 Circle the subordinating conjunctions, then write the subordinate clauses.

a It is the hardest thing in the world to frighten a mongoose because he is eaten up from nose to tail with curiosity. ______________________

b Rikki was a true mongoose although he looked like a cross between a cat and a weasel.
____

c A high summer flood washed him out of the burrow where he lived with his mother and father. ______________________

d He could fluff up his tail till it looked like a bottle-brush. ______________________
____

e Rikki-tikki climbed down to the floor where he sat rubbing his nose.
____

f If Teddy doesn't pick him up, he'll run in and out of the house all day long.
____

Try it out!

On a separate piece of paper, write as many sentences as you can by using a different **conjunction** in the blank space of the following sentence.

We took refuge in the hut ______________ *the wintry weather closed in.*

Black cockatoo

The hit came hard, sending the young *dirrarn* black cockatoo reeling from his roost in the large gum tree. The boy approached cautiously, shanghai dangling from his hand, to inspect his catch. The dirrarn lay sprawled amongst the smaller birds he'd been using as target practice.

"Jy! I hope you planning to eat that one, at least," said Mia, looking at the devastation at the bottom of the yard.

Jy whirled around, shanghai loaded. "Get lost, nobody asked you."

Mia bent down, scooped up the dirrarn, cradled it to her chest and walked defiantly back inside, tears in her eyes.

"We don't just kill for the fun of it, *jawiji* grandson," said Jy's grandfather, as he walked onto the verandah, cup of tea in hand. His calm presence insisted that he be heard.

"Nah, I was just practising, *jawiji* grandfather," Jy said, head bowed respectfully. "It was just some fun."

The grandfather slowly placed his tea on the back table and collected the dead birds from the ground. He threw all except one to the *gunyarr* dogs. "This one is your dinner," he said to his grandson. "Pluck and gut him before you bring him in."

Jy didn't argue, but when his jawiji walked inside he aimed his shanghai high and shot down a settled *wan.gura* crow from the tree in the neighbour's yard.

Inside the house Mia put the dirrarn into a dark cardboard box. She didn't know what had made her save this one, but she did. Growing up in the bush, she had seen many animals die and had hunted many of her own. She remembered the story her grandmother had told her about this bird, and that culturally she wasn't allowed to say its name or look at it. Seeing the red underwing flash brightly had drawn her attention to the dirrarn's small body sprawled out on the ground. She had been moved and had risked her brother's wrath by picking it up. She wasn't meant to challenge her brother; as her older brother she owed him a certain amount of respect. She wasn't even sure if the bird would survive. She could hear shallow breathing from within the box, so she knew it was alive. She placed the box carefully in her wardrobe, away from prying eyes, and went into the kitchen to join her mother and aunties getting the food ready for dinner.

Carl Merrison

A clause is a group of words that contains a verb. Main clauses can stand on their own as simple sentences. For example: *They grew fearful*. Subordinate clauses can be added to form complex sentences.
For example: *They grew fearful* ***when the reeds began to sway***.

1 Read the story "Black cockatoo". Use the coordinating conjunction *and* to join each pair of main clauses as one compound sentence, then find and underline the sentence in the extract.

a The grandfather slowly placed his tea on the back table. ________ He collected the dead birds from the ground.

b She had seen many animals die. ________ She had hunted many of her own.

A subordinate clause:
- always starts with a subordinating conjunction
- is not as important as the main clause in a sentence
- cannot stand alone as a sentence
- can be placed at the start, in the middle or at the end of a sentence.

2 Join the main clauses in Box A to the subordinate clauses in Box B to form complex sentences. Write them below.

A	B
Mia walked defiantly back inside	since she wanted to keep it away from prying eyes.
Jy didn't argue	when his *jawaji* walked inside.
She placed the box carefully in her wardrobe	although tears were in her eyes.

a ____

____

b ____

____

c ____

____

3 Underline the subordinate clauses in these complex sentences.

a She remembered the story her grandmother had told her about the bird, and that culturally she wasn't allowed to say its name or look at it.

b She placed the box carefully in her wardrobe, away from prying eyes, and went into the kitchen to join her mother and aunties getting the food ready for dinner.

Try it out!

On a separate piece of paper, add your own **subordinate clauses** to these **main clauses**.

a Mia bent down, scooped up the dirrarn ...

b The boy approached cautiously, shanghai dangling from his hand ...

Fabulous monsters 1

The Cyclops

The Cyclops (*say* **sye**-*klops*) were a hideous race of one-eyed giants.

They are usually portrayed as lawless, man-eating shepherds, although they had once helped the gods to forge fabulous armour and weapons. They had been responsible for supplying the chief god, Zeus, with his most fearsome weapons – lightning bolts and thunder.

One Cyclops, named Polyphemus, and a son of the sea god, Poseidon, trapped the hero Odysseus (*say oh*-**dee**-*see*-*us*) and his crew inside his cave using a huge boulder to block the entrance.

The monster then began eating the unfortunate men until Odysseus used trickery to outsmart him. The hero told Polyphemus that his name was Nobody. He used the giant's wine to get him in a drunken stupor and then, with the help of his crew, he sharpened a large wooden stake and used it to blind Polyphemus.

In furious pain, Polyphemus called out to his fellow Cyclops that Nobody had blinded him. The Cyclops, believing Polyphemus to be drunk, ignored his cries. Odysseus and his men strapped themselves to the giant's huge sheep. When Polyphemus removed the boulder from the cave entrance to allow the sheep out to pasture, the heroes managed to escape.

Scylla and Charybdis

Scylla (*say* **sill**-*a*) and Charybdis (say *kar*-**rib**-*dis*) were sister sea-monsters.

Scylla had 12 legs and six heads on long necks, and the mouths on each head contained three sets of terrible teeth. Some reports say that she also had several savage, howling and snapping dogs' heads attached to her waist. She lived inside a cave on the high cliffs above a narrow channel. She would stretch out as ships passed to seize and devour the helpless crew members.

As if this was not enough for sailors to fear, on the other side of the channel, lying in wait should ships try to steer clear of Scylla, was Charybdis.

Charybdis was an unusual monster in that she was never seen or described, because she lay below the sea's surface. As unsuspecting ships passed close by, she created a fantastic and deadly whirlpool which sucked whole ships down. Once the crews had been drowned, Charybdis spat them out in a huge watery spray.

Because the channel was so narrow, avoiding Charybdis usually meant sailing within reach of her dreadful sister Scylla.

A simple sentence contains one main clause and therefore only one verb. For example: *The monster **opened** its deadly eyes.* A compound sentence contains two or more main clauses and therefore two or more verbs. For example: *The monster **awoke** and the hero **approached**.* A complex sentence contains a main clause and one or more subordinate clauses and therefore two or more verbs. For example: *The monster **awoke** and **opened** its deadly eyes as the hero **approached**.*

1 Make compound sentences by joining the sentences with **and**, **but** or **so**.

a Scylla lived on the cliffs. Charybdis lived in the sea. ______

b Polyphemus had trapped the crew. They used trickery to escape. ______

c The ships tried to steer clear of the whirlpool. The channel was too narrow. ______

Here is a way to distinguish between types of sentences:
A **simple sentence** has only one verb. A **compound sentence** uses the coordinating conjunctions *and, but, so* and *or* to join two or more main clauses.
A **complex sentence** uses a subordinate conjunction to join a subordinate clause to a main clause.

2 Make complex sentences by joining the sentences using one of the conjunctions in the box.

although	because
until	before
which	when

a The Cyclops howled with pain. He had been blinded.

______

b Odysseus and his men were amazed. A one-eyed giant appeared.

______

c Cyclops are usually portrayed as lawless, man-eating shepherds. They had helped the gods to forge fabulous armour and weapons.

______

3 Circle any subordinating conjunctions and write whether the following are simple, compound or complex sentences.

a The Cyclops were a hideous race of one-eyed giants. ______

b The monster began eating the unfortunate men until Odysseus used trickery to outsmart him. ______

c Scylla had 12 legs and six heads on long necks, and the mouths on each head contained three sets of terrible teeth. ______

d The heroes managed to escape when Polyphemus removed the boulder from the cave entrance. ______

Try it out!

On a separate piece of paper, write a **simple sentence**, a **compound sentence** and a **complex sentence** on a subject of your choice.

The past

Let no one say the past is dead.
The past is all about us and within.
Haunted by tribal memories, I know
This little now, this accidental present
Is not the all of me, whose long making
Is so much of the past.

Tonight here in suburbia as I sit
In easy chair before electric heater,
Warmed by the red glow, I fall into dream:
I am away
At the camp fire in the bush, among
My own people, sitting on the ground,
No walls around me,
The stars over me,
The tall surrounding trees that stir in the wind
Making their own music,
Soft cries of the night coming to us, there
Where we are one with all old Nature's lives
Known and unknown,
In scenes where we belong but have
now forsaken.
Deep chair and electric radiator
Are but since yesterday,
But a thousand camp fires in the forest
Are in my blood.
Let none tell me the past is wholly gone.
Now is so small a part of time, so small a part
Of all the race years that have moulded me.

Oodgeroo Noonuccal

Commas are used:

- to show a pause in a sentence. For example: *Listen, can you hear the thunder?*
- to separate a list of adjectives that describe a noun. For example: *She wore a pretty, red, spotty hat.* (No comma is needed after the final adjective that comes before the noun.)
- to separate words in a list. For example: *You need to take a scarf, gloves, a coat and a hat.*
- to separate main and subordinate clauses in a sentence. For example: *My uncle, who lives in Barrambat, will be coming to Brisbane for his holiday.*

1 Write commas to separate clauses in the following sentences from the text.

a Let no one say the past is dead.

b The past is all about us and within.

c Haunted by tribal memories I know.

d Tonight here in suburbia as I sit.

2 Only one of the following sentences is correctly punctuated. Tick the box with the correctly punctuated sentence.

A I am away at the campfire in the bush among my own people sitting on the ground no walls around me the stars over me the tall surrounding trees that stir in the wind making their own music. ☐

B I am away at the campfire in the bush, among my own people, sitting on the ground. No walls around me the stars over me the tall surrounding trees that stir in the wind making their own music. ☐

C I am away, at the campfire in the bush among my own people, sitting on the ground. No walls around me, the stars over me, the tall surrounding trees that stir in the wind making their own music. ☐

D I am away at the campfire in the bush, among my own people, sitting on the ground. No walls around me, the stars over me, the tall surrounding trees that stir in the wind making their own music. ☐

3 Add commas, where needed, in the lines below.

a Haunted by tribal memories I know
This little now this accidental present
Is not the all of me

b In easy chair before electric heater
Warmed by the red glow I fall into dream

Try it out!

Draw lines to match each kind of **comma** use with an example.

Comma use	**Example**
to separate items in a list	*"Wait here, I'll fetch your coat."*
to show a pause	*Some children, the ones who had waited patiently, were rewarded with gold medallions.*
to separate clauses	*Before us lay a dark, dismal, ominous sky.*
to separate adjectives	*We saw tigers, lions, cheetahs, leopards and a panther.*

Unit 4.8 Quoted (direct) and reported (indirect) speech

Comic capers

A Big Nate

B Swaggles

C Peanuts

Quoted (direct) speech shows words that are actually spoken.
For example: *"Have you finished washing up yet?" asked Mum.*
The actual words spoken by Mum are placed inside speech marks.
Reported (indirect) speech is a report of what has been said.
For example: *Mum asked if I had finished washing up yet.*
Speech marks are not used for indirect speech.

1 Underline the words actually spoken (quoted speech) in the following dialogue.

"Doctor, doctor," complained the patient, "I can't remember anything!"

"How long has this been going on?" asked Dr Green.

"How long has what been going on?" answered the bewildered patient.

2 Rewrite the following exchange in quoted (direct) speech.

A reporter asked the captain of a container ship if there were any vegetables he preferred not to carry. The captain answered that he was reluctant to carry leeks on his ship.

Speech marks, inverted commas and quotation marks are all terms for the punctuation marks that enclose words that are actually spoken.
They can be single or double, but they should be used consistently.

3 Think of a joke or riddle you know as quoted (direct) speech and write it as if you were telling it to your best friend.

Try it out!

On a separate piece of paper, write "Comic capers" as both **quoted (direct)** and **reported (indirect) speech**.

Unit 4.9 Apostrophes of contraction

General knowledge quiz

Conduct research, if necessary, to help you find and write the answers to these questions.

1. Which sport would you be playing if you'd just made a strike of 10?

2. What won't a vegetarian eat?

3. Who out of the following wasn't an outlaw? Ned Kelly, Jesse James, Benjamin Franklin, Robin Hood, Ben Hall

4. Name the position of any player in a netball team who isn't allowed to score goals.

5. Which sportsperson would've achieved a Test match batting average of 100 if he had made just four more runs in his last Test?

6. Which character doesn't belong? Bluey, Chilli, Banjo, Peppa, Bandit

7. What's the name given to a person who assists a golfer?

8. Which of the following aren't crustaceans? crab, yabby, lobster, shark, seahorse, crayfish

9. Who of the following weren't musical composers? Ludwig van Beethoven, Lennon and McCartney, Johann Sebastian Bach, Laurel and Hardy, Queen Elizabeth I, Wolfgang Amadeus Mozart, Luke Skywalker

10. Name a film character that's associated with the expression, "To infinity and beyond!"

An apostrophe of contraction is used to show that one or more letters have been left out of a word.
For example: *can't = cannot*   *I'd = I would or I had*

1 Use the text opposite to help you write the contractions (shortened forms) of these words.

a would have ____________ **b** what is ____________

c are not ____________ **d** you had ____________

e is not ____________ **f** will not ____________

g was not ____________ **h** does not ____________

i were not ____________ **j** that is ____________

2 Write these contractions in full.

a you're ____________ **b** we've ____________

c it's ____________ **d** she'd ____________

e they'd ____________ **f** didn't ____________

g could've ____________ **h** don't ____________

i you'll ____________ **j** I'll ____________

3 Rewrite the sentences below, giving the contractions in full.

a "I've never seen such a beautiful sight and I wouldn't expect to ever see anything that could compare," said the enthusiastic traveller.

____

____

b "If you can't be at my house by 10," said Rasheed irritably, "then we'll just have to miss the start of the game."

____

____

c She'd searched everywhere but she still couldn't find the list he'd given her.

____

____

Try it out!

On a separate piece of paper, write sentences that clearly show the difference in the meaning of the following words.

a *it's and its* **b** *who's and whose* **c** *we're and were* **d** *you're and your*

Mixed-up possessions

Mickey Mouse's lightsaber

Thor's wand

Harry Potter's piano

Luke Skywalker's moonboot

Beethoven's hammer

Sherlock Holmes's ears

Neil Armstrong's hat

An apostrophe of possession is used to show that something belongs to a person or thing.
For example: *Erika's sword* = the sword belonging to Erika *The wind's howl* = the howl of the wind

1 The possessions of the characters on the opposite page have become mixed up. Rewrite the following list correctly using apostrophes of possession.

a ______________ ears **b** ______________ hammer
c ______________ wand **d** ______________ lightsaber
e ______________ piano **f** ______________ hat
g ______________ moonboot

When a word is singular, add an apostrophe and then add *s* whether the word ends in *s* or not.
For example: *The tractor's wheels were huge. James's dog is a collie.*

2 Rewrite using apostrophes of possession.

a the sails belonging to the ship ______________
b the bicycle belonging to Charles ______________
c the wail of the siren ______________
d the cry of the wolf ______________

The easiest way to remember where to place an apostrophe of possession is to ask who the owner is. Once you know the owner, place the apostrophe after the last letter of the owner's name.

When a word is plural, if it ends in *s* just add an apostrophe at the end of the word.
For example: *The horses' tails were swishing backwards and forwards.*

3 Rewrite using apostrophes of possession.

a the petals of the flowers ______________
b the petals of the flower ______________
c the buzz of the fly ______________
d the buzz of the flies ______________

When a word is plural but does not end in *s*, add an apostrophe and then *s*.
For example: *The women's meeting was held in the new hall.*

4 Complete the following.

a the children ________ game **b** the cattle ________ lowing
c the fish ________ habitat **d** the police ________ action
e the geese ________ feathers **f** the men ________ room

Try it out!

On a separate piece of paper, write the names of your family members – including pets – and your friends, as well as at least one possession they might have.
For example: *Mum's judo belt* *Sparky's rubber bone* *Sultan's saddle* *Antony's car*

Unit 4.11 Extension – Sentences and punctuation

Rangi and Papa
(A Maori legend)

In the beginning, Rangi the sky father and Papa the earth mother were so much in love that they hugged each other closely all the time.

When Rangi and Papa's children were born, they were trapped in the darkness of their loving parents' embrace. The children didn't like living in such darkness all of the time so they decided that they should try to escape into the light.

First Rongo, who was the eldest child, tried to push his parents apart. He pushed and pushed but it was no good because Rangi and Papa held each other too tightly.

Next Tangaroa tried. He heaved and pushed and strained, but he too failed to separate his parents. Each of the children took turns to separate their parents but without luck until finally it came to the youngest child, Tane, to try.

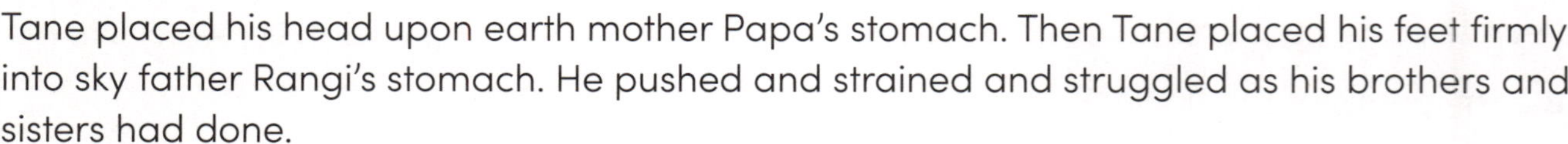

Tane placed his head upon earth mother Papa's stomach. Then Tane placed his feet firmly into sky father Rangi's stomach. He pushed and strained and struggled as his brothers and sisters had done.

Rangi the sky father cried out, "Stop, my son!" but Tane continued to push.

Papa the earth mother cried out, "Stop, my son!' but Tane continued to push.

Tane's parents began to shout and scream for they did not wish to be parted.

Slowly Tane began to stretch himself out and push his parents apart. Light started to stream into the world for the first time. The coming of light meant that plants began to grow.

Eventually Rangi and Papa were parted, but they were so sad that they both began to cry. They cried and cried and their tears became the rivers, the lakes and the sea. They cried so much that their children thought their parents would flood the new world. The children decided to roll Papa over for a short while each day so that Rangi couldn't see her. Once Rangi the sky father could no longer see his beloved wife, Papa the earth mother, he stopped crying.

Today, when you wake up each morning you can see Rangi's tears in the form of dewdrops, which he sheds at the first sight of his wife. When Papa sees Rangi for the first time each day she lets out loving sighs, which take the form of the early morning mists.

1 In each of the following sentences underline the **subject** in red and the **predicate** in blue.

- **a** Rongo tried to push his parents apart.
- **b** Tane's parents did not wish to be parted.
- **c** The tears became the rivers, lakes and the sea.

Remember, the **subject** is what is being talked about and the **predicate** is what is being said about the **subject**.

2 Circle the **verb** in brackets that agrees with the **subject**.

- **a** The children (was/were) trapped between their parents.
- **b** Tane (is/are) pushing and straining with all his might.
- **c** Their tears (become/became) the rivers, lakes and the sea.

3 Rewrite the following sentence elements to form one sensible sentence.

placed (**verb**) Tane (**subject**) into Rangi's stomach (**phrase**) his feet (**object**)

____

4 Circle the **subordinating conjunction** in each of these sentences.

- **a** The children of Rangi and Papa were trapped because of their loving parents' embrace.
- **b** Tane pushed and strained until he separated Rangi from Papa.
- **c** The children of Rangi and Papa loved their parents, although they wished for more light.

5 Tick the sentence below that is punctuated correctly.

- **a** First Rongo who was the eldest child tried to push his parents apart.
- **b** First Rongo who was the eldest child, tried to push his parents apart.
- **c** First Rongo, who was the eldest child, tried to push his parents apart.
- **d** First, Rongo who was the eldest, child tried to push his parents apart.

6 Rewrite the following reported speech as **direct (quoted) speech**.

Rangi cried out that he wanted his son Tane to stop.

____

Try it out!

On a separate piece of paper, rewrite the following using **apostrophes of possession** where necessary.

- **a** the stomach of Rangi
- **b** the children of Rangi and Papa
- **c** the efforts of the children
- **d** the tears of their parents

Topic 4: Test your grammar

Sentences, clauses, conjunctions, direct and indirect speech and apostrophes

1 Shade the bubble next to the **subject** of the following sentence.

The sheep dog slowly circled the stray lambs.

- ○ The sheep dog
- ○ slowly
- ○ circled
- ○ the stray lambs

2 Shade the bubble next to the **subject** of the following sentence.

The mayor announced excitedly that Toby was the winner.

- ○ The mayor
- ○ announced excitedly
- ○ announced excitedly that Toby was the winner.
- ○ Toby was the winner

3 Shade the bubble next to the correct answer and then write the answer in the box.

*A **subordinate clause** can only be found in a* ______ .

- ○ simple sentence
- ○ compound sentence
- ○ complex sentence
- ○ phrase

4 Shade the bubble next to the word that would correctly complete this sentence.

The singers ______ *singing the national anthem.*

- ○ is
- ○ are
- ○ am
- ○ was

5 Shade the bubble next to the word that would correctly complete this sentence.

Ally and Cam ______ *eating ice cream.*

- ○ like
- ○ likes
- ○ lick
- ○ liking

6 Shade the bubble next to the **object** in the following sentence.

Captain Swish carried the treasure chest.

- ○ Captain Swish
- ○ carried
- ○ the treasure chest
- ○ carried the treasure chest

7 Shade the bubble next to the **prepositional phrase** in the following sentence.

The scout troop met at Black Dog Reserve.

- ○ The scout troop
- ○ met
- ○ at Black Dog Reserve
- ○ The scout troop met

8 Shade the bubble below the **coordinating conjunction** in this sentence.

The girls had finished but the boys were still working.

○ had ○ but ○ were ○ still

9 Shade the bubble next to the **subordinating conjunction** that would best join these sentences.

Harriet suspected the goblin was inside. The door was open.

○ where ○ until ○ although ○ because

10 Mark where **commas** belong in this sentence.

The bear cub which had been slumbering peacefully awoke with a fright.

11 Shade the bubble next to the correctly punctuated sentence.

○ "Aren't you going to watch Perry's performance?" asked Coby's friend Tim.

○ Aren't you going to watch Perry's performance? "asked Coby's friend Tim."

○ "Are'nt you going to watch Perry's performance?" asked Coby's friend Tim.

○ "Aren't you going to watch Perrys' performance?" asked Cobys' friend Tim.

12 Shade the bubble that shows the **fleece of a sheep**.

○ a sheeps' fleece ○ a sheeps fleece ○ a sheep's fleece ○ a sheep fleece

13 Shade the bubble next to the **contraction** of **they are**.

○ there ○ theyr'e

○ their ○ they're

How am I doing?

Tick the boxes if you understand.

A simple sentence contains one main clause made up of a subject and a predicate. ☐

The subject and verb of a sentence must agree. ☐

Coordinating and subordinating conjunctions are used to join clauses and simple sentences. ☐

Sentences can be simple, compound or complex. ☐

Commas can separate clauses in a sentence. ☐

Topic 5: Using grammar to enrich your writing

Learning intention

We are learning about the different grammatical features we find in informative, imaginative and persuasive texts.

Unit 5.1 Using grammar in informative texts (explanation)

Thunder and lightning

Do you know why we don't hear and see thunder and lightning at the same time? Read on to find out ...

Thunder is the sound lightning makes. Sound is made up of vibrations. These vibrations move through the air until they reach the ear. For us to be able to hear thunder, lightning must cause vibrations.

We know that lightning is a huge discharge of electricity. When this discharge takes place, the electricity hits the air and the air starts to vibrate. Lightning is also incredibly hot. The lightning heats up the air around it. Then the air expands because it is hot. This expanding air causes another vibration. These vibrations together bounce off clouds or the ground, causing the sound we hear as thunder.

The reason that we don't hear and see thunder and lightning at the same time is because light travels much faster than sound. This means that when you hear thunder the lightning that caused it has already occurred.

Cause	Effect
Lightning makes sound.	We hear thunder.
Vibrations move through the air.	The sound reaches our ear.
The vibration bounces off the air or the ground.	This causes the sound of thunder.
Light travels faster than sound.	We don't hear thunder and see lightning at the same time.

Facts about thunder and lightning

- Lightning can reach temperatures of 30 000°C, which is five times hotter than the surface of the Sun.
- Lightning strikes upwards as well as downwards.
- A stroke of lightning can be more than 30 kilometres long.
- Ball lightning is a really weird kind of lightning. It appears as a fiery, red, yellow or orange sphere, about the size of a grapefruit, which floats a metre or so above the ground.
- Scientists still don't fully understand how lightning works.

Let's look at the way grammar is used in an **informative text**. Informative texts, such as the explanation opposite, generally use a lot of complex sentences to explain how something happens or the reason why something occurs. A complex sentence contains a main clause and a subordinate clause starting with a subordinating conjunction.

Subordinate clauses can be added, where appropriate, to the start, the end or sometimes the middle of a main clause.

For example: *Then, the air expands **because** it is hot.*
*Then, **because** it is hot, the air expands.*
***Because** it is hot, the air expands.*

Some common subordinating conjunctions include **because**, **if**, **when**, **since**, **until** and **while**.

1 Read "Thunder and lightning". Use the explanation on the opposite page to help you rewrite the following complex sentences, placing the subordinate clause in an alternative place.

a Lightning must cause vibrations for us to be able to hear thunder.

____

b Because light travels faster than sound, we don't hear thunder and see lightning at the same time.

____

____

2 Write three subordinating conjunctions that are used in the text to join clauses.

__________ __________ __________

Informative texts, such as explanations, often include relating verbs written in the timeless present tense to show that the actions or states of being are continuous, always happening or always true. For example: *Thunder is the sound lightning makes.*

3 Write two sentences from the text that are written in the timeless present tense.

____

____

4 Write any relating verbs used in the sentences you wrote in question 3.

____

____

5 Write three examples of technical nouns used in the text.

__________ __________ __________

Try it out!

Select one of the topics below and, on a separate piece of paper, write an explanation of your own, making sure you include **complex sentences**, **timeless present tense**, **relating verbs** and **technical nouns**.

Topics:
- How paper is made
- How a drone works
- Believe it or not!

You keep runnin'

"You keep runnin', you'll only go to jail tired," Ben Silver muttered.

He hit the photo button on his battered video camera and took another picture. He reached across his forest set and moved the legs on two small clay figures. Ben was eye-level with the action, peering between trees made from cellophane and toilet rolls and other found things.

He often mumbled his characters' lines as he shot a movie. Later, after he'd filmed everything, he would record the voices and add them to the pictures. He jotted the line in his brown leather notebook:

"You keep runnin', you'll only go to jail tired."

Ben took a bite from a microwaved jam doughnut. The jam was lava on his tongue and he dropped the doughnut onto the plate. The floor around him was littered with clothes, shoes, a game console, two controllers, a bike wheel with no tyre, a skateboard deck, schoolbooks, soccer boots, a jumbo-size packet of chips and plates from long-forgotten afternoon snacks. Ben's favourite place. It was dark with the curtains closed, the only light coming from two lamps trained on the stop-motion set on his desk. Outside, his dog Golden barked like mad.

Within the Woods was Ben's seventh stop-motion movie. In this scene a zombie thief named Dario Savini was running down a forest track with Detective Ben Silver, Sydney's toughest cop, in pursuit. The detective was famous in Ben's movies for vanquishing werewolves, delinquent kids and zombies.

There was a heavy knock.

"Hello. Police!"

Ben froze. He looked at his clay cop, but clay Ben just stood there on one foot, mid-stride, frozen.

Another heavy knock on the front door. It definitely didn't sound like Olive. She was in the backyard, playing pirates on the trampoline like she did every day after school.

Ben stood, walked quietly out of his bedroom and tiptoed up the hall, heart keeping time with his footsteps. He moved through the lounge room to the front window and peered carefully from behind the dusty grey curtain.

It was raining and two police officers were huddled under the front awning. One fat. One skinny. Skinny was a lady. A couple of police cars were parked on the kerb with two more cops standing under dark blue umbrellas next to one of the cars. Ben's body surged with excitement and fear. His dream was to become a detective once he had finished high school.

Ben's little sister came in through the broken sliding back door, soaking wet. "Who is it?" Olive asked.

"Shhh," he whispered, raising a hand to tell her to stop, but Olive kept coming. She was small, whiteblonde, seven years old, one of the smartest kids Ben knew. She had already read *The Hobbit* by herself. For three weeks afterwards she refused to speak unless people called her Gandalf.

The knock again. The lady officer walked past the window. Ben tucked himself in behind the curtain. The officer disappeared around the side of the house.

Olive shuffled in front of Ben. "Police!" she said in a too-loud voice. He placed his hand over her mouth. She peeled it off. "They're coming to get you for what you did."

from *Two Wolves* by Tristan Bancks

Let's look at the way grammar is used in an **imaginative text**. Imaginative texts, such as "Two wolves" opposite, use paragraphs to organise information. In this particular narrative, the author uses each paragraph to expand descriptions of the characters and settings.

1 Read the story and then write a label that could be used to describe the main subject or topic of each of the following paragraphs.

For example: *Second paragraph* *Ben's filming process*

a Third paragraph ______________________________

b Fifth paragraph ______________________________

c Sixth paragraph ______________________________

d Eighth paragraph ______________________________

Prepositional phrases often feature in imaginative texts to sharpen ideas and develop a fuller description of the details about how, when and where things are taking place.

2 Complete the sentences below with prepositional phrases from the story. Beside each sentence, write whether the phrase tells **how**, **when** or **where**.

a Ben hit the photo button ______________________________

b ______________________________ he would record the voices and add them to the pictures.

c Two police officers were huddled ______________________________

d Ben's body surged ______________________________

The authors of imaginative texts often play with language to entertain their audience. In this case, Tristan Bancks has used detailed descriptions, saying verbs, a simile and even a metaphor to entertain his audience.

3 A metaphor is a figure of speech that compares something or someone to something else as if it were that thing. Write the metaphor describing the jam on Ben's tongue.

____

4 Underline the sentences that highlight Ben's emotional state.

5 Rewrite the sentence below, replacing the saying verb in bold with the more specific verb used in the story to show the impact of a different saying verb on the tone and mood of a sentence.

*"Shhh," he **said**, raising a hand to tell her to stop, but Olive kept coming.*

"Shhh," he __________, raising a hand to tell her to stop, but Olive kept coming."

Try it out!

On a separate piece of paper, write a news article about the events happening in the story. Imagine you are a reporter covering the incident at Ben's house. Include quotes from characters and describe the scene.

Ned Kelly – Hero or villain?

Recently, an article appeared on the *Nor'easter News* site about the bushranger Ned Kelly. A number of people responded in the comments section, debating whether the outlaw was an Australian hero or villain. Here is the latest reply to the article …

I must comment on your article about whether Ned Kelly was a hero or a villain, because all the facts definitely point to Ned Kelly being a villain. Let me cite some facts.

First, as a teen, Kelly was an apprentice to Harry Powers, which sounds commendable, until you become aware that Powers was a horse thief! The young villain went on to become accomplished at stealing horses, at the same time establishing a reputation around north-east Victoria as a bare-knuckle brawler. This makes him a thief and a thug.

Second, let me remind you of the indisputable fact that Kelly and his sidekicks were responsible for the cold-blooded murder of three police officers at Stringybark Creek. Kelly, after stealing the watch from the dead Sergeant Kennedy, is quoted as saying, "What's the use of a watch to a dead man?" This surely leaves no doubt that Kelly was a remorseless murderer.

Then, there is the siege at the Glenrowan Hotel in which Kelly and his gang of thugs held innocent civilians hostage. Around the same time, the gang attempted to derail a train carrying police troops and their horses. This makes Kelly a nineteenth-century terrorist.

Next, let us not forget that in the lead-up to the siege at Glenrowan, Kelly had despatched Joe Byrne to murder his boyhood friend and suspected police informer, Aaron Sherritt. Sherritt was unarmed and with his wife and newly born babe when Byrne gunned him down. This makes Kelly and Byrne vengeful bullies.

In summary, let the facts speak for themselves. Rather than set Ned Kelly high up on that hero's pedestal to be worshipped and adored, we really should be remembering him for exactly what he was – a notorious and villainous killer.

Prof. J. S. Providence (Melbourne, Australia)

Let's look at the way grammar is used in a **persuasive text**. Persuasive texts, such as the one opposite, are generally organised in paragraphs. The first paragraph is used to introduce the argument and state the writer's position.

1 Read the first paragraph of "Ned Kelly – Hero or villain?" (after the opening statement). Circle the word or words in the first paragraph that show the writer's position in this argument. Do they want to persuade you that Ned Kelly is a hero or a villain? ______

The paragraphs following the opening statement are generally used to present a series of arguments, often with topic sentences that start with text connectives to link the arguments in each paragraph. For example: *First, ...*

2 Read the rest of the reply to the article and then write the text connectives used to link the paragraphs.

______

3 Write one example of a topic sentence used to introduce the main idea of a paragraph.

______

In this persuasive text, the writer has carefully selected specific noun groups to portray the main character in a negative light to further persuade the audience of his point of view.

4 Write the noun groups in each paragraph that are used to describe Ned Kelly.

First paragraph: *a villain* ______

Second paragraph: ______

Third paragraph: ______

Fourth paragraph: ______

Fifth paragraph: ______

Concluding paragraph: ______

5 Write the antonym for *villain* used in contrast to Ned Kelly. ______

6 Write two modal adverbs used on the opposite page. ______

Try it out!

Write a blog post about someone you regard as a hero. Use specific **noun groups** to portray your hero in a positive manner in order to persuade your audience that he or she is deserving of an award.

OR: Argue one side or discuss both sides of one of the following arguments:

- Should professional sport be played on Anzac Day?
- Is climate change real?
- Chicken farming – caged or free range?

Topic 5: Test your grammar

Punctuation

1 Shade the bubble next to the missing punctuation mark to complete the sentence.

What a fantastic hat

○ .   ○ ?   ○ !   ○ ,

2 Shade the bubble next to the missing punctuation mark to complete the sentence.

We travelled from Cairns to Brisbane

○ .   ○ ?   ○ !   ○ ,

3 Shade the bubble next to the missing punctuation mark to complete the sentence.

Where did you find your locket

○ .   ○ ?   ○ !   ○ ,

4 Shade the bubble next to the correctly punctuated sentence.

○ Is the city with the largest population in england london.

○ Is the city with the largest population in England, London?

○ Is the city with the largest population in England, London.

○ Is the city with the largest population in england, London?

5 Shade the bubble next to the correctly punctuated sentence.

○ The rainbow's colours are violet, indigo, blue, green, yellow, orange and red.

○ The rainbow's, colours are violet indigo blue green yellow orange and red.

○ The rainbow's colours are, violet indigo blue green yellow orange and red.

○ The rainbow's, colours, are, violet, indigo, blue, green, yellow, orange and red.

6 Shade the bubble next to the correctly punctuated sentence.

○ Magda who had only just arrived sat down next to Sadie.

○ Magda, who had only just arrived, sat down next to Sadie.

○ Magda who, had only just arrived, sat down next to Sadie.

○ Magda who had only just arrived, sat down next to Sadie.

7 Shade the bubble next to the correctly punctuated sentence.

- ◯ Look out shouted Tom who had been watching Mel with interest.
- ◯ Look out "shouted Tom!" who had been watching Mel with interest.
- ◯ "Look out!" shouted Tom, who had been watching Mel with interest.
- ◯ "Look out!" shouted Tom, "who had been watching Mel with interest."

8 Use the correct punctuation to rewrite this sentence in the box.

A flat long hard throw is much better than a high soft one explained our coach

9 Add commas, where they belong, in this sentence.

The dancers who had been rehearsing for weeks performed splendidly.

10 Shade the bubble next to the correctly punctuated sentence.

- ◯ "Hey, let's eat Grandad!"
- ◯ "Hey, let's eat, Grandad!"
- ◯ "Hey let's eat Grandad!"
- ◯ "Hey let,s eat Grandad!"

How am I doing?

Tick the boxes if you understand.

I understand how grammar is used in informative, imaginative and persuasive texts. ☐

I understand how to use grammar to enrich and improve what I write. ☐

Topic 6: Enrichment and revision

Learning intention

We are learning to use language devices to expand our vocabulary and we are learning how to edit our writing.

Unit 6.1 Prefixes and suffixes

Fabulous monsters 2

The Lernean Hydra

From Greek mythology, the Hydra was a huge serpent living in the Lernean Swamp. The monster had many heads (some say seven and some say nine), each of which breathed poisonous breath. The Lernean Hydra was confronted by the courageous hero Heracles, who found that when he lopped one head from the massive creature, two more grew in its place. To overcome the problem of multiple heads growing, Heracles used a torch to seal each neck stump shut so no further heads could grow.

One of the heads, however, was immortal and, upon lopping it from the creature's neck, Heracles imprisoned it beneath a massive rock. There it may very well be even today.

The Kraken

Scandinavian mythologies tell us of a huge, tentacled sea monster resembling a giant squid. It is said to be so large that it can be mistaken for a small island. Spending most of its time slumbering in the deepest parts of the ocean, the Kraken occasionally awakens, stirs and arises to the surface to attack ships by wrapping its massive tentacles around vessels and crushing them or dragging both them and their crews down into the murky depths.

It is thought that the stories about the Kraken are based on the sightings of real giant squid which, although not the size of small islands, are still capable of wrestling a sperm whale and capsizing a small fishing boat.

Prefixes are word parts that change the meaning of words when added to the beginning of another word or word part.

For example: *inter-* means "between" or "among" (*intersect, internet, intermediate*)

1 Add prefixes from the box to the words or word parts to form new words.

tele- *fore-* *anti-* *mono-*

a __________ clockwise **b** __________ plane **c** __________ leg

d __________ scope **e** __________ phone **f** __________ head

g __________ nuclear **h** __________ rail **i** __________ vision

2 Add prefixes to the following words to make them antonyms (opposites).

a __________ visible **b** __________ fortunate **c** __________ appear

d __________ knowingly **e** __________ perfect **f** __________ behave

g __________ responsible **h** __________ legal **i** __________ sense

Suffixes are word endings. When some suffixes are added to nouns or verbs, they usually form adjectives.

For example: *break + able = breakable, sense + ible = sensible, glory + ous = glorious*

3 Use suffixes or prefixes to change the following nouns to adjectives.

a poison __________ **b** mortal __________

c remark __________ **d** courage __________

4 Write your own words that can begin with the following prefixes.

a ***tri-*** *(meaning three)* __________

b ***bi-*** *(meaning two)* __________

c ***auto-*** *(meaning self)* __________

____

Try it out!

The **suffix** *-ist* means "person who does". Write eight words ending in *-ist* that describe people who do things. For example: *artist* (someone who works in any of the arts). On a separate piece of paper, write a sentence for each word.

__________ __________ __________ __________

__________ __________ __________ __________

The shark

He seemed to know the harbour,
So leisurely he swam;
His fin,
Like a piece of sheet-iron,
Three-cornered,
And with a knife-edge,
Stirred not a bubble
As it moved
With its base-line on the water.
His body was tubular
And tapered
And smoke-blue,
And as he passed the wharf
He turned,
And snapped at a flat-fish
That was dead and floating.
And I saw the flash of a white throat,
And a double row of white teeth,
And eyes of metallic grey,
Hard and narrow and slit.
Then out of the harbour,
With that three-cornered fin,
Shearing without a bubble the water
Lithely,
Leisurely,
He swam –
That strange fish,
Tubular, tapered, smoke-blue,
Part vulture, part wolf,
Part neither – for his blood was cold.

E. J. Pratt

OXFORD UNIVERSITY PRESS

While a strong knowledge of grammar is very important, it is also important for us to widen our **vocabulary** so that we can enrich our writing while using correct grammar.

1 Use the poem on the opposite page and the parts of speech listed below to help you find interesting words that mean the following.

a *(adverb)* at a relaxed and easy pace ______

b *(verb)* slicing through ______

c *(adjective)* shaped like a tube ______

d *(common noun)* a scavenging bird of prey ______

e *(adjective)* like metal ______

f *(verb)* agitated ______

g *(noun)* place where boats dock ______

h *(adjective)* triangular ______

2 Use a dictionary to help you write clear definitions for these words.

a lithely ______

b tapered ______

c dorsal fin ______

3 Write words from the poem that are **antonyms** for these words.

a alive ______ **b** sinking ______

c wide ______ **d** frantically ______

e easy ______ **f** wide ______

Try it out!

The words in the box below are all **abstract nouns** of emotion.

Circle the **abstract nouns** that you think best describe how the poet felt about the shark.

alarm	boredom	fear	love	pity	sorrow
anger	depression	fury	nervousness	sadness	terror
apprehension	embarrassment	interest	panic	shame	wonder
awe	excitement	jealousy			

Jordy's postcard

Jordy has been travelling in the wilds of Canada. After a close encounter, he decided to be a bit old-fashioned and send a postcard to Rema, his friend in Australia. Unfortunately, Jordy didn't pay much attention in his English classes back home. Can you decipher what he has written on his postcard home?

Deer rema,

Isle bee home soon.

Your knot going two believe watt Im going too tell yew. Yesterday in the woulds near the creak I sore too bares. Won was a mail I think because he had grate big pause. Anyways, both the bares clause was huge. I thought they had mist seaing me but suddenly the won I thought was a mail let out a whale and rushed strait four me. Luckily I was able two seas hold of a low bow and swing up into a nearby beach tree. That bare beet the trunk with his pores but I scrambled hire and was safe. I no in future daze to come ill take moor care when im bye myself. I is looking forward to catching up and sharing sum other storeys with ewe when I return to australia in a few weaks thyme.

Youre good friend jordy.

1 As you have seen, Jordy's postcard needs a little bit of work before it can be easily read.

Edit Jordy's postcard for him by rewriting it below. Look out for homonyms, incorrect contractions and poor punctuation.

Frog saunas

Chytrid is a fungal disease, and frogs are at the top of the list of potential victims.

At the bottom of a closed quarry next to Sydney Olympic Park is the frontier of the fight to save ...* the endangered green and golden bell frog. One of the largest remaining populations in the state lives at the old brickpit ...

"This is great habitat for the frogs to breed in, for tadpoles to grow up in," Dr Anthony Waddle from Macquarie University said. There are also artificial pond systems that have been put in and these are where we find the majority of the frogs ...

Dozens of small greenhouses dot the landscape, each containing a tower of black-painted masonry bricks. These will help to save the frogs from the killer chytrid fungus, which has been linked to the extinction of 90 frog species around the world.

It's a simple solution built from basic things bought from a hardware warehouse. The greenhouses are known as "frog saunas" because of the way they heat up in sunlight.

Chytrid is at its most deadly in the winter. Combating the fungus requires a solution that is inviting for the frogs and keeps them warm.

As it happens, standard masonry bricks have "frog-sized" holes in them, as Dr Waddle describes them, and the greenhouses warm them up when in contact with direct sunlight.

In Dr Waddle's research published in the journal *Nature*, frogs were not only attracted to the saunas but also became more resilient to chytrid and were resistant to subsequent infections.

"We found that if you can simply keep the frogs a bit warm in winter you can prevent them from dying. Having high humidity and heat is really key to attracting the frogs and also getting rid of their chytrid infections." ...

Brick houses

It's a fitting new chapter in the history of bricks, many of which were made in the same pit the research is taking place in.

It's also a fitting new chapter for the area, which was spared from development before the 2000 Sydney Olympics when the endangered frogs were discovered at the site ...

He is pleased by how widely his work has spread, connecting him with fans including a pottery club on the NSW South Coast looking to make frog saunas in their area.

He is encouraging the public to get involved and has published an online guide of how to build the saunas ... You can help frogs this winter by building "frog saunas".

Declan Bowring, ABC News

*The ellipses indicate that some text from the original article has been omitted.

1 Circle the three common nouns in this sentence.

Frogs have survived on our planet longer than humans.

2 Circle the two adjectives in this sentence.

The fungal disease chytrid has been attacking small vertebrates.

3 Circle the verbs or verb groups in these sentences.

a Frogs are at the top of the list of potential victims.

b Dozens of small greenhouses dot the landscape.

c This area was spared from development.

4 Circle the adverb in this sentence.

Dr Waddell is pleased by how widely his work has spread.

5 Rewrite the following sentences as one sentence using a conjunction to join them. In your new sentence, replace any repeated common nouns with suitable pronouns.

Frogs disappearing is alarming for all of us.
It is known that what affects frogs also affects humans.

6 Underline the prepositional phrase in this sentence.

Small greenhouses have been placed on the site.

7 Write commas where they belong in the following sentence.

As it happens standard masonry bricks have "frog-sized" holes as Dr Waddle describes them and the greenhouses warm them up when in contact with direct sunlight.

Try it out!

Rewrite the **reported (indirect) speech** of scientist Dr Waddle on the opposite page as **quoted (direct) speech** using the correct punctuation.

Time to reflect

Tick each box when you are confident that you understand and can use the grammar listed when you write.

Understand	Use	Grammar and punctuation focus
☐	☐	I select specific common, proper, collective or abstract nouns to represent people, places, animals, things and ideas.
☐	☐	I choose suitable nouns to fit the topic of my writing or to represent different characters or settings.
☐	☐	I use a range of adjectives to describe characters and settings.
☐	☐	I know how to expand noun groups with articles and a variety of adjectives for fuller descriptions.
☐	☐	I use thinking and feeling verbs to express opinions.
☐	☐	I use modal verbs such as **could**, **would**, **should** and **must** to help persuade my audience.
☐	☐	I choose suitable doing, saying or relating verbs to report facts or entertain the reader.
☐	☐	I can use present, past and future tense verbs correctly.
☐	☐	I use adverbs and prepositional phrases to make interesting sentences with details about where, when, how or why something happens.
☐	☐	I use antonyms (opposites) and synonyms (words with a similar meaning) to help describe and compare people, places, animals, things or ideas.
☐	☐	I use pronouns that agree with the noun to which they refer. For example: **Evie/she**, **the boys/they**
☐	☐	I know how to use text connectives to link paragraphs or sentences in time or sequence. For example: **first**, **then**, **later**, **finally**
☐	☐	I use paragraphs to organise my writing into logical bundles.
☐	☐	I use topic sentences to introduce the main idea in each paragraph.
☐	☐	I sometimes use similes and metaphors in my writing to describe and compare subjects or to develop a character or setting.
☐	☐	I understand that idioms have a different meaning from the actual words used.

Understand	Use	Grammar and punctuation focus
☐	☐	I understand that the subject and verb in a sentence must agree.
☐	☐	I know how to use coordinating conjunctions (**and**, **but**, **so**, **or**) to make a compound sentence.
☐	☐	I know how to use the subordinating conjunctions (for example: **if**, **because**, **until**, **when**) to join a main clause to a subordinate clause.
☐	☐	I know the difference between simple, compound and complex sentences.
☐	☐	I use commas in lists correctly most of the time.
☐	☐	I recognise how quotation marks are used in quoted (direct) speech.
☐	☐	I understand the difference between quoted (direct) and reported (indirect) speech.
☐	☐	I understand that an apostrophe of contraction can be used to show where a letter is missing in a shortened word.
☐	☐	I understand how to use an apostrophe of possession to show ownership.
☐	☐	I understand the difference between informative, imaginative and persuasive texts.

Glossary

adjective	A word that describes a noun: *red, old, large, round, three* **comparative adjective** (compares two things): *stronger* **positive adjective** (in simplest form): *strong, good* **possessive adjective** (shows possession and comes before a noun): *my, your, his, her, its, our, your, their* **superlative adjective** (compares more than two things): *strongest, best, most enjoyable*
adverb	A word that usually adds meaning to a verb to tell when, where or how something happened: *slowly, immediately, soon, here* **modal adverb** (shows degree of certainty): *definitely, probably*
antonym	An opposite: *full/empty, sitting/standing, front/back*
apostrophe of contraction	A punctuation mark that shows where a letter (or letters) is missing in a **contraction** (shortened word): *isn't, we'll*
apostrophe of possession	A punctuation mark that shows ownership: *Ali's hat, the woman's car, the students' backpacks*
clause	A unit of grammar that usually contains a subject and a verb. There are **main clauses** and **subordinate clauses**. *When Peter called out, I looked around.*
comma	A punctuation mark used to separate items in a list, to show a short pause or to separate a main clause and a subordinate clause. *Mum, can I go? When I leave, I will take some apples, bananas, oranges and cherries.*
coordinating conjunction	A joining word used to join two simple sentences or main ideas: *and, but, so, or*
homonym	A homonym can be a homograph or a homophone: **homographs** words with the same spelling but different meaning: *saw* (a tool), *saw* (past tense of *see*) **homophones** words that sound the same but are spelled differently: *sun/son*
metaphor	A figure of speech that compares something or someone to something else as if it were that thing: *the night was a cloak; the grapefruit moon*
noun	A word that names people, places, animals, things or ideas. Nouns can be: **abstract nouns** (things that cannot be seen or touched): *happiness, idea* **collective nouns** (names of groups): *team, flock, bunch, herd* **common nouns** (names of ordinary things): *hat, toys, pet, mouse, clock, bird* **concrete nouns** (things that can be seen or touched): *book, pet, boy, girl*

	proper nouns (special names): *Max, Perth, Friday, March, Easter, Australia* **technical nouns** (sometimes called scientific nouns): *oxygen*
noun group	A group of words, often including an article, one or more adjectives and a noun, that build on a main noun: *the strange old house*
object	The person or thing that has the action of the verb done to them
paragraph	A section of text containing a number of sentences about a particular point. Each paragraph starts on a new line.
phrase	A group of words that adds details about when, where, how, why: *after lunch, with a spoon, for Olivia*
plural	More than one: *chairs, dishes, boxes, cities, donkeys, loaves, foci*
predicate	What is being said about the thing or person (subject) in a sentence.
prefix	A word part that, when added to the beginning of another word or word part, changes the meaning: ***dis**appear, **mis**behave*
preposition	A word that usually begins a prepositional phrase: *on, in, over, under, before*
prepositional phrase	A group of words that starts with a preposition and adds details about when, where, how, why: *in the car, after lunch, with a spoon, for Olivia*
pronoun	A word that can take the place of a noun to represent people, places, animals, things or ideas: *he, she, I, it* **first person pronoun**: *I, me, mine, we, us, ours* **possessive pronoun**: *mine, his, hers, ours, yours, theirs* **relative pronoun**: *who, whom, whose, which, that* **second person pronoun**: *you, yours* **third person pronoun**: *he, him, his, she, her, hers, it, its, they, them, theirs*
quoted (direct) speech	The direct speech that someone actually says. Quoted speech uses **quotation marks** at the start and end of the actual words spoken.
reported (indirect) speech	The indirect speech reporting what someone else has said
sentence	A group of words that makes sense, and includes a subject and at least one verb. A **simple sentence** has one main idea or main clause and one verb or verb group: *The birds **were sitting** on the fence.* A **compound sentence** uses coordinating conjunctions (*and, but, or, so*) to join two main clauses. A compound sentence has two verbs or verb groups: *Some birds **were sitting** on the fence and a cat **was lurking** below.* A **complex sentence** uses subordinating conjunctions to join a main clause with one or more subordinate clauses. A complex sentence has two or more verbs or verb groups: *The tiger snake **eats** birds, although frogs **are** its preferred prey.*

Glossary *continued*

simile	A figure of speech used to compare two things using the words *like* or *as*: *like a bird; as red as a beetroot*
subject	The noun or noun group naming who or what a sentence is about.
subordinating conjunction	A joining word used to join a main clause and one or more subordinate clauses: *because, since, when, if*
suffix	A word ending. It often changes the part of speech of a word: *grace* (abstract noun) – *graceful* (adjective)
synonym	A word that means the same or nearly the same as another word: *shouts/yells, thin/skinny*
text connective	A signpost word or group of words that tells how the text is developing – generally used to link two sentences or paragraphs: *First, Second, Next, However, For instance*
topic sentence	A sentence, usually placed at the start of a paragraph, that introduces the main point being made in the paragraph.
verb	A word that tells us what is happening in a sentence. Verbs can be: **auxiliary verbs** (helping verbs used with a main verb): ***is** going, **could** go* **compound verbs** (made up of a helper, or auxiliary, and main verb): *is sitting* **doing verbs**: *walked, swam* **modal verbs** (telling how sure we are about doing something): *should, could, would, may, might, must, can, will, shall* **relating verbs**: *am, is, are, had* **saying verbs**: *said, asked* **simple verbs** (one word): *went* **thinking and feeling verbs**: *know, like*
verb group	A group of words that build on a main verb: *might have been wondering* (in this example, *wondering* is the main verb)
verb tense	Refers to time and tells whether the action or process is in the present, past or future: *runs/is running, thought/was thinking, will help* **timeless present tense**: Used when the action is continuous: *Flies are insects.*